Adorable Sock Dolls to Make & Love

Connie Stone • Emola Lowe

Sterling Publishing Co., Inc. New York
A Sterling/Chapelle Book

Chapelle:

- Owner: Jo Packham

- Editor: Karmen Quinney

- Staff: Marie Barber, Ann Bear, Areta Bingham, Kass Burchett, Rebecca Christensen, Holly Fuller, Marilyn Goff, Shirley Heslop, Holly Hollingsworth, Sherry Hoppe, Shawn Hsu, Susan Jorgensen, Pauline Locke, Barbara Milburn, Linda Orton, Leslie Ridenour, Cindy Stoeckl

- Photography: Kevin Dilley/Hazen Photography

- Photostylist: Peggy Bowers

- Scenery for photography: Sherry Ferrin and Anita Louise Crane

Library of Congress Cataloging-in-Publication Data

Stone, Connie.
    Adorable sock dolls to make & love /
Connie Stone, Emola Lowe.
        p.   cm.
    "A Sterling/Chapelle book."
    Includes index.
    ISBN 0-8069-3795-5
    1. Dollmaking. 2. Cloth dolls. 3. Socks
I. Lowe, Emola. II. Title.
TT175.S76 1999   98-40057
745.592'21—dc21   CIP

10 9 8 7 6 5 4 3 2 1

A Sterling/Chapelle Book

First paperback edition published in 2000 by
Sterling Publishing Company, Inc.
387 Park Avenue South, New York, N.Y. 10016
Produced by Chapelle Ltd.
P.O. Box 9252, Newgate Station, Ogden, Utah 84409
© 1999 by Chapelle Limited
Distributed in Canada by Sterling Publishing
℅ Canadian Manda Group, One Atlantic Avenue, Suite 105
Toronto, Ontario, Canada M6K 3E7
Distributed in Great Britain and Europe by Cassell PLC
Wellington House, 125 Strand, London WC2R 0BB, England
Distributed in Australia by Capricorn Link (Australia) Pty Ltd.
P.O. Box 6651, Baulkham Hills, Business Centre, NSW 2153, Australia

Printed in China
All rights reserved

Sterling ISBN 0-8069-3795-5 Trade
            0-8069-3693-2 Paper

If you have any questions or comments or would like information on specialty products featured in this book, please contact: Chapelle Ltd., Inc., P.O. Box 9252 Ogden, UT 84409 (801) 621-2777 • FAX (801) 621-2788 • E-Mail Chapelle1@ AOL.Com

About the Authors

The authors, Emola and Connie, are a mother-daughter team that has been crafting together for more than 20 years. They started by making crafts for their homes. Family and friends saw their crafts and wanted them for their own homes. So, instead of making just two craft projects, they ended up making dozens for family and friends. Eventually, they started a small craft business, Heart to Art, which sells their finished projects and craft supplies. With their projects in great demand, they are kept very busy.

Emola is a retired youth corrections supervisor. She has four daughters, of which Connie is the youngest. Emola has 20 grandchildren, 41 great grandchildren, and two great, great grandchildren.

Connie has been married to her husband, Tom, for 30 years. They have three children, Tom Jr., Tami, and Tyson. She has three grandchildren, Justin, Kelsey, and Skyler.

Their partnership has been a wonderful experience. Not only are they mother and daughter, they are also best friends. Emola and Connie plan to keep making creations and running their craft business for years to come.

Dedication

We would like to thank everyone at Chapelle for their help, especially Jo, Becky, and Areta. Many thanks to our families for being so patient and understanding, especially Tom.

Contents

Carefully read and follow all of the general instructions and the directions within the project pertaining to the specific sock doll. The colors of socks used in this book are simply suggestions. Substitute any color(s) desired.

Choosing Socks

The texture and weave of socks play an important role in creating sock dolls. Stretchy socks hold more stuffing and work best for enlarged features and large sock dolls (see Mr. Gorilla on page 17). Most cotton socks are stretchy. Socks with a smooth texture, do not stretch much, and are great for faces and hands. Nylon socks are smooth textured and work best for small projects (see Baby Buddies on pages 68-69). Socks are available trimmed with lace and embellishments. Embellished socks save time (see Kelsey and Tiny Dancer on page 71).

Make certain to feel the sock and stretch it both ways. If large gaps appear between the threads, polyester stuffing will show through. Also, stretch across the ribbing to get an idea of what the finished sock doll will look like. Some ribbing becomes flat when stretched or stuffed with polyester stuffing, while others stay tight.

As an alternative, turn socks inside out. This can give your project an entirely new and even more desirable look (see Chicken on page 42 and Mr. Shivers on page 86).

From this point, you will never look at socks again without imagining the possibilities (a pair of green socks as a bug or Martian; red and black socks as a lady bug; or blue as a whale). Discount stores have the lowest prices, but sometimes the quality is compromised. Specialty sock stores

have the widest and most interesting variety. Sizes range from babies' to men's. All of the sock dolls in this publication have been made from women's socks size 9-11 unless stated otherwise.

There are several styles, such as anklets, crew, tube, and knee-highs. One style of sock cannot be replaced by another style of sock. For example, an anklet sock cannot be used when a tube sock is called for in the materials list because an anklet is much smaller than a tube and there will not be enough sock to create the sock doll. Have fun checking out various stores for project ideas.

Tips:

- Experiment with various colors, sizes, and textures on each project.

- Try turning socks inside out. It is amazing how different a project can look by experimenting. There is no right or wrong look.

- Use your creativity.

Diagrams

Cutting lines on diagrams are used to show the general area in which to cut the sock. Measurements are given only in specific instances and may be adjusted as needed. The area between "X" marks on diagrams should be left open.

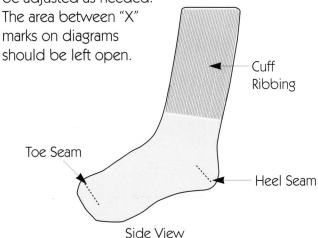

Toe Seam

Cuff Ribbing

Heel Seam

Side View

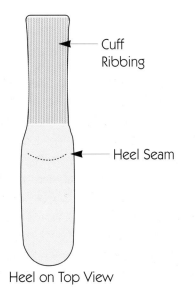

Cuff Ribbing

Heel Seam

Heel on Top View

Cutting

The following items are necessary for cutting socks into desired pieces: fabric marker, fabric scissors, socks, and straight pins.

1 Using fabric marker, mark cutting lines clearly onto socks.

2 Using straight pins, pin sock through both layers to secure.

3 Using fabric scissors, make clean, precise cuts. Avoid small jagged cuts.

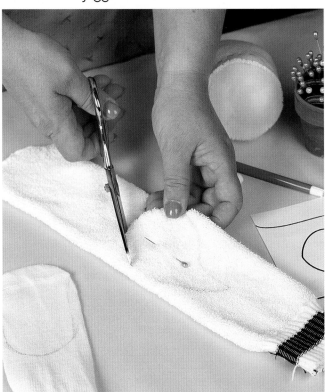

Most of the socks used will need to lay flat on their side for marking and cutting as shown in Side View. However, some project instructions call for the the sock to lay with the heel on top as shown in Heel on Top View and photo on top left on opposite page. Make certain to pin sock through both layers so that the sock does not move.

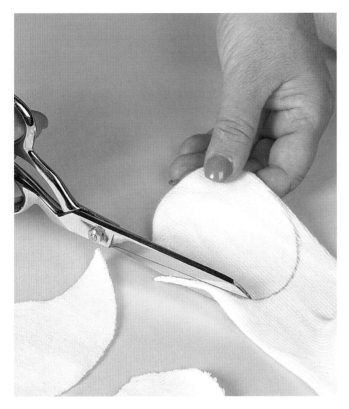
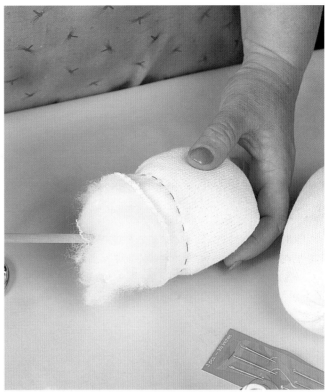

Sewing

All seam allowances are ¼". Any sewn seams with excess sock should be cut close to seam. Remember that there are no hard-and-fast rules to apply. The fabric will dictate some of the decisions about seam allowances because of its stretchability, and fraying tendencies. <u>All sewing is done with a 3" doll needle and carpet thread unless specified otherwise.</u>

Stuffing

A good quality polyester stuffing is recommended for stuffing the sock doll. Purchase a stuffing tool or a ¼"-wide dowel to push stuffing into areas that fingers cannot reach. Some projects need to be stuffed more firmly than others. Legs used for standing require firm stuffing to support the sock doll's weight. Bellies and noses require firm stuffing to stand out.

Tips:

- Take time to stuff the sock doll properly.

- Use small pieces of stuffing.

- Stuff pieces lightly that need to remain soft and moveable.

- Stuff heads firmly so that they feel hard.

Sculpting

Sculpting gives a flat surface character, definition, and dimension. Doll or sculpting needles are used for sculpting. Most sculpting is done with a 3" needle; however, a 5" needle is used for projects that require going through the head and neck. Carpet thread, matching the sock color, is recommended. *Note: Contrasting carpet thread has been used in the photographs for easy illustration of techniques.* For each area sculpted, use a 24" length of carpet thread. Repeat stitching back to front or side to side until desired shape is achieved.

Sculpting Eyes

1 Thread 3" doll needle with carpet thread. Knot end. Using fabric marker, place two small marks for eye placement, remembering that sculpting will set the eyes closer together.

2 Push needle through mark on right side and out left side. Pull thread tight. Push needle back through left side and out right side. Pull thread tight. Repeat until desired shape is achieved.

3 Pull thread tight. Knot. Push needle back through and cut thread, hiding thread inside sock.

Sculpting Mouth through Head & Neck

1 Thread 5" doll needle with carpet thread. Knot end. Using fabric marker, place small marks for mouth placement.

2 Push needle through back of neck, out right side of mouth, back through right side of mouth and out back of neck, back through neck, and out

next to previous stitch. Pull tight. Repeat until mouth is desired length and shape.

3 Pull thread tight. Knot. Push needle back through and cut thread, hiding thread inside sock.

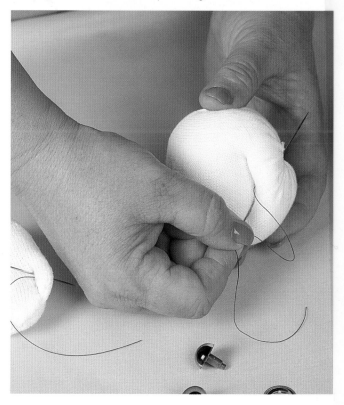

Sculpting Mouth Horizontally

1 Thread 3" doll needle with carpet thread. Knot end. Using fabric marker, place small marks for mouth placement.

2 Push needle through end of mark on right side and out left side. Pull thread tight. Push needle back through left side and out right side next to previous stitch. Pull thread tight. Repeat until desired shape is achieved.

3 Pull thread tight. Knot. Push needle back through and cut thread, hiding thread inside sock.

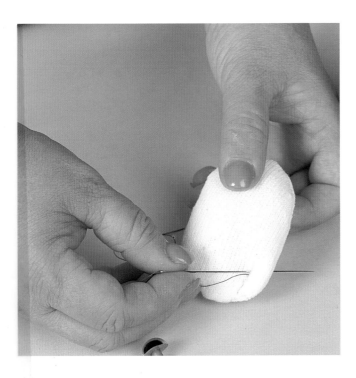

Sculpting Toes, Fingers & Hooves

1 Thread 3" doll needle with carpet thread. Knot end.

2 See Loop Stitch on page 12. Make desired length Loop Stitch for each toe or finger. Pull tight to shape.

3 Pull thread tight. Knot. Push needle back through and cut thread, hiding thread inside sock. Repeat for amount of toes, fingers, and hooves required.

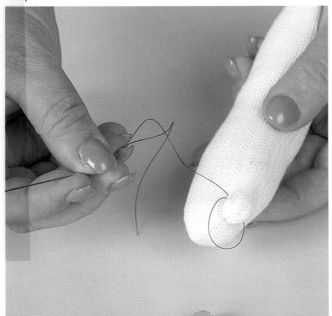

Proportions

Check construction of doll regularly to make certain that proportions are right for the finished sock doll.

Tips:

- Make certain that the head is not too big or too small for the rest of the body.

- Make certain the torso is about the same length as the legs. (Some sock dolls do have longer legs to create a special effect.)

- Make certain the tips of the hands are above midthigh. (Some sock dolls do have longer arms to create a special effect.)

Child-Safe 🤍

When making any of these sock dolls for children under the age of three, please read all instructions carefully. Take the child's age and abilities into consideration when making a sock doll as a gift.

Safety eyes can be used on projects for ages three and up. These eyes have a plastic shank protruding from the back with a metal or plastic disk fitting over the shank to keep eyes in place.

Embroidered and felt eyes and noses are recommended for sock dolls that will be given to children under the age of three. See Attaching Eyes and Attaching Noses on pages 10-11. All child-safe sock dolls in this publication are marked with the following symbol: 🤍

Safety Tips:

- Avoid embellishments that are small enough to swallow. If embellishments are added, sew securely to sock doll.

- Avoid using glue. Many types are considered toxic.

- Avoid all types of beaded eyes, mouths, or noses.

Attaching Eyes

There is a wide variety of eyes to choose from, such as bead, button, embroidered, felt, glass, plastic, and safety.

Safety Eyes

1 Using fabric marker, place two small marks for eye placement on face. Sculpted eye area is already done.

2 Push plastic shank through fabric where marked. If sock is a tight weave, it may be necessary to cut a very small slit for the shank to go through. Place disk onto shank and push almost halfway up.

Embroidered Eyes

1 Using fabric marker, place two small marks for eye placement on face. Sculpted eye area is already done.

2 See Cross-stitch, French Knot, or Satin Stitch on pages 12-13. Using embroidery needle and floss, embroider eyes on face.

Felt Eyes

1 Using fabric marker, place two small marks for eye placement on face. Sculpted eye area is already done.

2 Using fabric scissors, cut two eyes in desired shape from felt. Place eyes over marked areas. See Running Stitch on page 13. Sew eyes on face.

Craft Eyes

1 Using fabric marker, place two small marks for eye placement on face. Sculpted eye area is already done.

2 Adhere eyes of choice onto face with craft glue. If using safety eyes, cut off shanks near base before gluing. Remember this technique is not child-safe.

Attaching Noses

There is a wide variety of noses to choose from, such as button, embroidered, felt, plastic, and safety. Embroidered, felt, or safety noses are recommended for sock dolls that will be given to young children.

Safety Nose

1 Using fabric marker, place nose placement on face. Sculpted nose area is already done. Some noses will be affixed above a sculpted area.

2 Push plastic shank through fabric where marked. If sock is a tight weave, it may be necessary to cut a very small slit for the shank to go through. Place disk onto shank and push almost halfway up.

Embroidered Nose

1 Using fabric marker, place nose placement on face. Sculpted nose area is already marked. Some noses will be applied above a sculpted area.

2 See Cross-stitch or Satin Stitch on pages 12-13. Using embroidery needle and floss, embroider nose on face.

Felt Nose

1 Using fabric marker, place nose placement on face. Sculpted nose area is already done. Some noses will be affixed above a sculpted area.

2 Using fabric scissors, cut nose in desired shape from felt. Place nose over marked area. See Running Stitch on page 13. Sew nose on face.

Craft Nose

1 Using fabric marker, place nose placement on face. Sculpted nose area is already done. Some noses will be affixed above sculpted area.

2 Adhere nose of choice onto face with craft glue. If using safety nose, shank can be cut off near base before gluing. Remember this technique is not child-safe.

Attaching Mouths

Mouths for the projects in this book are made from shaped wire or sewn with embroidery floss or thread.

Embroidered mouths are recommended for sock dolls that will be given to young children. Mouths can be sewn with Loop Stitch, Running Stitch, or Stem Stitches. See Stitches on pages 12-13 for the desired stitching technique.

Embroidered Mouth

1 Using fabric marker, place mouth placement on face. Sculpted mouth area is already done.

2 See Loop Stitch, Running Stitch, or Stem Stitch on pages 12-13. Using embroidery needle and floss, sew mouth on face.

Attaching Body Parts

When attaching body parts, turn raw edge of body part in ¼", and attach in place with Ladder Stitch on page 12. An additional row of stitching may be required to achieve desired look.

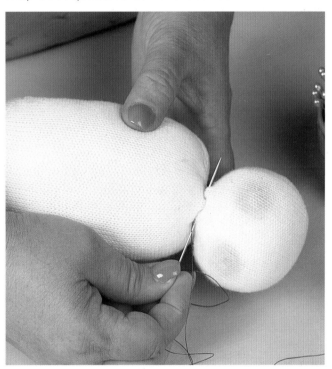

Blushing

Paintbrushes that are small and worn (½" or less) work well for blushing. Larger paintbrushes do not allow as much control when applying blush to a sock doll. The bristles of worn paintbrushes are spread out from prior usage, giving blushed area a softer look. Face blush or a piece of chalk can be used for blush.

1 Using paintbrush, brush lightly back and forth on blush to load.

2 Brush lightly on a paper towel to remove excess blush.

3 Brush lightly back and forth on cheeks. Repeat if darker shade is desired. It is better to repeat than to apply too heavily. The blush will not come off once applied. Do not try to remove with water.

Stitches

Cross-stitch

1 Bring needle up at A; go down at B, forming a diagonal straight stitch.

2 Bring needle up at C; go down at D, crossing the first stitch with an equal-sized diagonal straight stitch.

3 Repeat as needed.

French Knot

1 Bring needle up at A; smoothly wrap thread once around needle (more if desired).

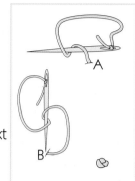

2 Hold thread securely off to one side and go down at B next to starting point.

3 Completed French Knot.

Gather Stitch

1 Knot thread. Bring needle up at A; go down at B, following a straight line.

2 Pull thread tightly while, pushing fabric toward knot.

3 Repeat as needed.

Ladder Stitch

1 Knot thread. Bring needle up at A; go down at B on joining edge.

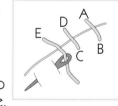

2 Bring needle across ¼" and up at C; go down at D on first edge. Bring needle across ¼" and up at E. Pull tightly.

3 Repeat as needed.

Loop Stitch

1 Bring needle up at A; go outward around cusp to starting point. Bring needle up at A again, two or three times. Pull tightly.

2 Repeat as needed.

Running Stitch

1 Bring needle up at A; go down at B, following a straight line.

2 Repeat as needed.

Satin Stitch

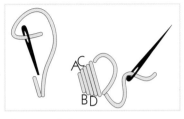

1 Keep thread smooth and flat. Bring needle up at A; go down at B, forming a straight stitch. Bring needle up at C, next to A. Go down at D, next to B, forming another straight stitch next to the first.

2 Repeat as needed.

Stem Stitch

1 Bring needle up at A. Keeping thread to left and below needle, go down at B. Up at C.

2 Repeat as needed.

Materials & Tools

The materials and tools listed below will be needed in most projects:

Materials

Carpet thread: for sculpting faces

Craft glue: for adhering eyes, mouths, noses, and embellishments

Embroidery floss: for eyes, mouths, noses, and embellishing, recommended for children under the age of three

Felt: for child-safe eyes, mouths, noses, and embellishing, recommended for children under the age of three

Polyester stuffing: for stuffing sock dolls

Safety eyes: for child-safe eyes (They have a locking disk that holds them in place, and are recommended for children over the age of three.)

Safety noses: for child-safe noses (They have a locking disk that holds them in place, and are recommended for children over the age of three.)

Sewing thread: for stitching and tacking as instructed

Socks: for sock doll body and clothes

Wire: for buttons, mouths, and embellishing

Tools

Craft scissors: for cutting cardboard, paper, and plastic

Doll needles: 3" for basic stitching, tacking, and side to side sculpting; 5" for sculpting noses and mouths through head and neck (Sculpting needle is a suitable substitute.)

Embroidery needle: for embroidering eyes, mouths, and noses

Fabric marker: for marking patterns (including openings) on socks; eye, mouth, and nose placement on face (A disappearing fabric marker is recommended.)

Fabric scissors: for cutting fabrics

Needlenose pliers: for holding small parts in place

Paintbrush: ½"-wide or smaller for applying blush to designated areas on sock dolls

Ruler: for measuring pattern pieces, circumferences, and diameters (Measuring tape is a suitable substitute.)

Straight pins: for holding socks in place when cutting and keeping pieces together when stitching

Stuffing tool: for pushing polyester stuffing into tight areas and to shape pieces

Wire cutters: for cutting pieces of wire and shanks from backs of safety eyes and noses

At the Zoo

Alligator ♥

(Photo on page 15.)
Materials & Tools on page 13
Blush
Socks: 1 pair, crew, green, for body

Instructions

1 Begin by reading General Instructions on pages 5–13. Stitches and special techniques used are explained in the General Instructions.

2 Organize all materials and tools needed for project. Using fabric marker, mark cutting lines onto socks as shown in Diagrams A–B.

3 Using fabric scissors, cut out marked pieces from socks. Body, head, and tail are one piece. Cuff of sock is tail and heel of sock is head. Total length is 13".

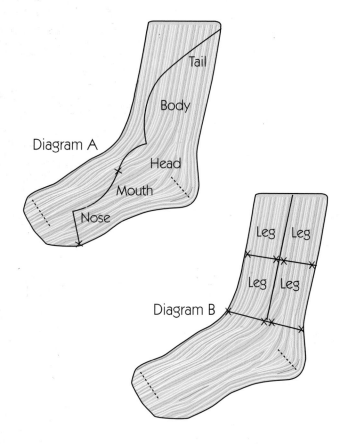

Diagram A

Diagram B

Head, Body & Tail

4 Fold body piece in half lengthwise, with right sides together. Sew along raw edge 11½" from tail to mouth with Running Stitch, leaving open where marked.

5 Turn right side out. Stuff from tail to mouth with polyester stuffing. Seam will be on belly.

6 Sew over Running Stitch with Ladder Stitch.

7 Sculpt eye area at heel seam. Attach safety eyes to sculpted area.

8 Stuff from mouth to tip of nose with polyester stuffing.

9 Sew front of mouth closed with Ladder Stitch. Sew 1½" line on each side of mouth with Ladder Stitch to define mouth.

10 Sculpt heel of sock vertically between eyes with one long Loop Stitch to define top of head and eyes. See photo on page 15.

Legs

11 Fold each leg piece lengthwise, with right sides together. Sew lengthwise along raw edge with Running Stitch, leaving open where marked.

12 Create three toes on one end of each leg with Running Stitch as shown in Diagram C. Using fabric scissors, cut away excess sock between toes.

Diagram C

13 Turn right side out. Stuff with polyester stuffing.

14 Sew legs to body with Ladder Stitch. Make certain toes are facing out.

Finish

15 Using small paintbrush, brush blush lightly on cheeks and mouth.

Mr. Gorilla 💜

(Photo on page 17.)

Materials & Tools on page 13

Socks: 1 pair, crew, black, for muzzle, ears, hands, and feet; 1 pair, crew, dk. brown speckled, for body

Instructions

1 Begin by reading General Instructions on pages 5–13. Stitches and special techniques used are explained in the General Instructions.

2 Organize all materials and tools needed for project. Using fabric marker, mark cutting lines onto socks as shown in Diagrams A–D.

3 Using fabric scissors, cut out marked pieces from socks.

Head

4 Sew along raw edge with Gather Stitch. Pull slightly to gather, leaving unsecured.

5 Stuff firmly with polyester stuffing.

6 Sculpt eye area of face. Attach safety eyes to sculpted area.

7 Pull gather to close. Knot to secure.

Muzzle

8 Sew around opening with Gather Stitch. Pull slightly to gather, leaving unsecured.

9 Stuff firmly with polyester stuffing. Toe seam is mouth.

10 Attach safety nose to top center of muzzle down ¼" frow raw edge.

11 Pull gather to close. Knot to secure.

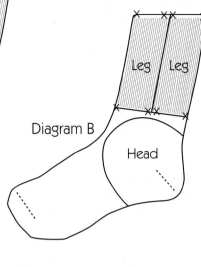

Diagram A

Diagram B

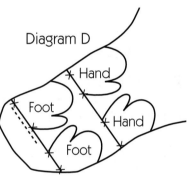

Diagram C

Diagram D

Note: Cut 1¼" above toe seam for muzzle.

Note: Cut ear piece on fold to open.

12 Sew muzzle to face with Ladder Stitch.

Ears

13 Fold each ear piece, with right sides together. Sew along raw edge with Running Stitch, leaving open where marked.

14 Turn right side out. Sew across opening with Gather Stitch. Pull gather to close. Knot to secure.

15 Sew gathered edge of ear to head with Ladder Stitch. Fold top of ear down and sew to head through fold with Running Stitch.

Body

16 Stuff firmly with polyester stuffing until desired shape is achieved. See photo on page 17.

17 Sew around opening with Gather Stitch. Pull gather to close. Knot to secure.

18 Sew gathered end of head to body with Ladder Stitch.

Arms & Legs

19 Fold each arm and leg piece lengthwise, with right sides together. Sew lengthwise along raw edge and across one end with Running Stitch, leaving open where marked.

20 Turn right side out. Stuff firmly with polyester stuffing.

Hands & Feet

21 Fold each hand and foot piece, with right sides together. Sew along raw edge with Running Stitch, leaving open where marked.

22 Turn right side out. Stuff firmly with polyester stuffing.

23 Place open ends of hands and feet over sewn ends of arms and legs. Sew in place with Running Stitch, ¼" in from raw edge of hands and feet.

24 Sew arms and legs to body with Ladder Stitch.

25 Fold leg and arm band pieces with outer edges to the center. Sew with Gather Stitch, leaving unsecured.

26 Place bands around seam where hands and feet are sewn to arms and legs. Pull threads tightly to gather. Knot to secure. Tack bands to arms and legs.

Mrs. Gorilla

(Photo on page 20.)
Materials & Tools on page 13
Blush
Ribbon: ⅝"-wide (10")
Ribbon roses: miniature (4)
Socks: 2 pairs, crew, cream speckled, for body;
   1 pair, crew, pink, for sweater

Instructions
   Assemble Mrs. Gorilla according to Mr. Gorilla's instructions including Diagram A and the additional instructions below. *Note: Mrs. Gorilla does not have leg or arm bands.*

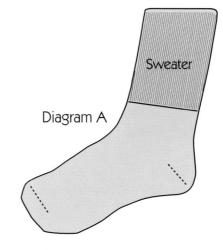

Diagram A

Note: Cut across both pink socks as shown in Diagram A. Cut one side of each tube to open for sweater.

Sweater

1 Place sweater pieces, with right sides together. Sew from finished edge down one side with Running Stitch.

2 Place sweater around gorilla, with finished edge as bottom of sweater and seam in back. Using fabric marker, mark two arm holes on sweater, leaving 1½" above neck for collar.

3 Using fabric scissors, cut two small slits where marked. Turn right side out. Place sweater on gorilla. Turn top of sweater down, forming collar. Tack in place. Trim with ribbon roses.

Finish

4 Using small paintbrush, brush blush lightly on cheeks, mouth, and inside ears.

5 Wrap ribbon around head for headband. Tack to secure. Adhere ribbon rose to headband with craft glue.

Dinosaur ♥

(Photo on page 22.)

Materials & Tools on page 13

Blush

Socks: 1 pair, crew, med. green, for body; 1 sock, crew, dk. green, for scales

Instructions

1 Begin by reading General Instructions on pages 5–13. Stitches and special techniques used are explained in the General Instructions.

2 Organize all materials and tools needed for project. Using fabric marker, mark cutting lines onto socks as shown in Diagrams A–C.

3 Using fabric scissors, cut out marked pieces from socks. Head, body, and tail are one piece.

Head, Body & Tail

4 Sew around sock approximately 4" from toe end to form head and neck with Gather Stitch.

5 Stuff head firmly with polyester stuffing until desired shape is achieved. See photo on page 22.

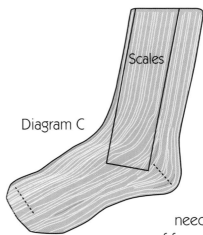

Diagram C

6 Pull to gather, leaving unsecured.

7 Sculpt eye area of face. Attach safety eyes to sculpted area.

8 Using 5" doll needle, sculpt mouth area of face, using toe seam as mouth, by pushing needle through mouth and out back of neck, through neck and out mouth next to previous stitch. Repeat until mouth is desired length and shape.

9 Pull gather on neck to close. Sew over Gather Stitch on neck with Ladder Stitch.

10 Stuff body firmly with polyester stuffing.

11 Sew opening closed with Ladder Stitch.

Legs

12 Fold each leg piece lengthwise, with right sides together. Sew lengthwise along raw edge of each leg with Running Stitch, leaving open where marked.

13 Place a sole piece inside end of each leg, with right sides together. Sew around edges with Ladder Stitch.

14 Turn right side out. Stuff firmly with polyester stuffing.

15 Sew around sole end of each leg with Loop Stitch, forming a foot.

16 Sew legs to body with Ladder Stitch.

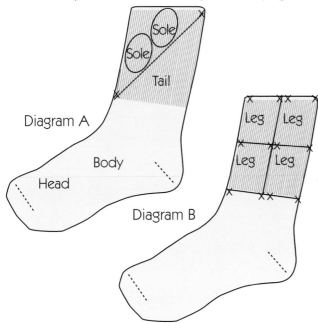

Diagram A

Diagram B

Scales

17 Fold scales lengthwise, with wrong sides together. Using fabric marker, mark scales as shown in Diagram D. Using fabric scissors, cut scales.

Fold

Diagram D

18 Fold scales lengthwise, with right sides together. Sew along raw edge with Running Stitch, leaving open where marked as shown in Diagram D.

19 Turn right side out. Sew scales to center of back from neck to tail with Ladder Stitch.

Finish

20 Using small paintbrush, brush blush lightly on cheeks and mouth.

Bears

(Photo on page 24.)

Materials & Tools on page 13 (for one bear)
Blush
Fabric: 1"-wide (16")
Socks: 1 pair, crew, brown, for body

Instructions

1 Begin by reading General Instructions on pages 5–13. Stitches and special techniques used are explained in the General Instructions.

2 Organize all materials and tools needed for project. Using fabric marker, mark cutting lines onto socks as shown in Diagrams A–B.

3 Using fabric scissors, cut out marked pieces from socks.

Head & Face

4 Sew around opening with Gather Stitch. Pull slightly to gather, leaving unsecured.

5 Stuff firmly with polyester stuffing until desired shape is achieved. See photo on page 24.

6 Sew defining lines on face with Running Stitch as shown in Diagram C.

7 Sculpt eye area of face. Attach safety eyes to sculpted area.

8 Pull gather to close. Knot to secure.

Diagram C

Muzzle

9 Fold muzzle, with right sides together. Sew a ¼" x 1" dart with Running Stitch as shown in Diagram D.

10 Open muzzle and sew around raw edge with Gather Stitch. Pull to gather while stuffing to desired size with polyester stuffing. Knot to secure.

Diagram D

11 Attach safety nose to muzzle.

12 Sew muzzle to face with Ladder Stitch.

Ears

13 Stuff lightly with polyester stuffing.

14 Sew across openings with Gather Stitch. Pull slightly to gather. Knot to secure.

15 Sew ears to head with Ladder Stitch.

Body & Legs

16 Fold body and leg piece with heel seam up and with right sides together. Sew up 2½" from leg end, then four stitches across to form crotch, and down other side with Running Stitch, as shown in Diagram E, leaving open where marked. Cut between seams.

Continued on page 25.

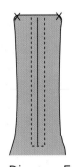

Diagram E

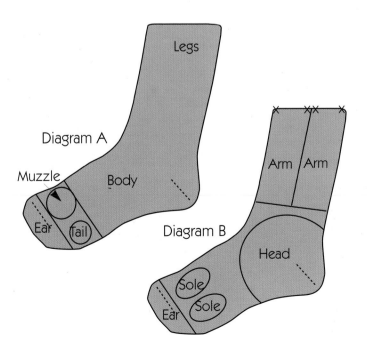

Diagram A

Diagram B

Within these walls an Angel sings of ABC's and learning new things

Continued from page 23.

17 Place a sole piece inside end of each leg, with right sides together. Sew around edges tightly with Ladder Stitch.

18 Turn right side out. Stuff legs firmly to the top of each leg with polyester stuffing.

19 Sew across leg tops with Running Stitch as shown in Diagram F.

Diagram F

20 Stuff body firmly with polyester stuffing.

21 Sew around opening with Gather Stitch. Pull gather to close. Knot to secure.

22 Sew head to body with Ladder Stitch. Tack bears legs to body with Ladder Stitch, making legs face forward.

Arms

23 Fold each arm piece lengthwise, with right sides together. Sew lengthwise along raw edge with Running Stitch, leaving open where marked.

24 Place a sole piece inside end of each arm, with right sides together. Sew around edge tightly with Ladder Stitch.

25 Turn right side out. Stuff firmly with polyester stuffing.

26 Sew arms to body with Ladder Stitch.

Tail

27 Sew around edge of circle with Gather Stitch. Pull gather to close. Knot to secure.

28 Sew tail to bottom of body with Ladder Stitch.

Finish

29 Using small paintbrush, brush blush lightly on cheeks, nose, soles, and inside ears.

30 Wrap fabric strip around neck. Tie into bow. Tack to secure.

Angelic Bear

(Photo on page 26.)
Materials & Tools on page 13
Blush
Button: miniature
Doilies: 5"-dia., scalloped, cream (2)
Embroidery floss: pink (6")
Pearls: wire strand, 4 mm
Socks: 1 pair, crew, cream, for wings; 1 pair, crew, pink, for body
Wire: 19-gauge, gold

Instructions

Assemble Angelic Bear according to Bears' instructions on page 23 and the additional instructions below.

Sweater

1 Place center of one doily on top of arm and let drape over arm, body, and neck as shown in Diagram A.

Diagram A

2 Sew "sleeve" seams together on underside of arm. Repeat process with remaining doily on other arm. Randomly tack sweater to body. Doilies will not fit around entire back of bear.

3 Turn neck edge down, forming collar. Turn each sleeve edge up, forming cuff.

4 Sew button onto front of sweater. Tie embroidery floss into small bow and tack to front of sweater to secure. See photo on page 26.

Finish

5 Shape wired pearls into halo. Attach halo to gold wire. Tack wire to back of body.

6 See Wings on page 95. Make wings.

7 Adhere wings to back of bear with craft glue, covering back edges of sweater and wire.

8 Using small paintbrush, brush blush lightly around top edge of wings.

Giraffe ♥

(Pictured above at left.)
Materials & Tools on page 13
Blush
Socks: 1 sock, crew, brown, for mane and antlers;
  1 pair, crew, brown and cream tie-dyed, for
  body; 1 sock, crew, red, for collar

Instructions

1 Begin by reading General Instructions on pages 5–13. Stitches and special techniques used are explained in the General Instructions.

2 Organize all materials and tools needed for project. Using fabric marker, mark cutting lines onto socks as shown in Diagrams A-B.

3 Using fabric scissors, cut out marked pieces from socks.

Head & Neck

4 Fold head and neck piece, with right sides together. Sew along raw edge with Running Stitch, leaving open where marked.

27

Note: Ear pieces should be 1½" on all sides.

Diagram A

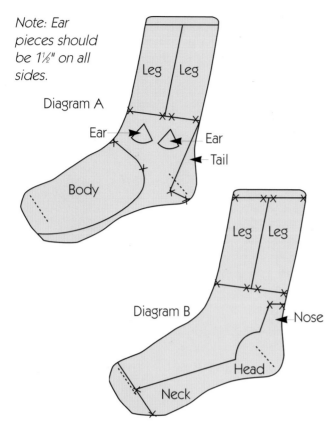

Leg Leg

Ear — — Ear

— Tail

Body

Diagram B

Leg Leg

— Nose

Head

Neck

5 Turn right side out. Stuff firmly with polyester stuffing.

6 Sculpt eye area of face. Attach safety eyes to sculpted area.

7 Turn end of nose in and sew around ¼" from end with Gather Stitch. Pull gather to close. Knot to secure.

8 Sculpt mouth area of face.

Ears

9 Turn bottom edges to middle. Tack to secure.

10 Sew tacked end of ears to head with Ladder Stitch.

Body

11 Turn body piece, with right sides together.

Sew along raw edge with Running Stitch, leaving open where marked.

12 Turn right side out. Stuff firmly with polyester stuffing.

13 Sew around opening with Gather Stitch. Pull gather to close. Knot to secure.

14 Align seams of neck and body. Sew neck to body with Ladder Stitch.

Legs

15 Fold each leg piece lengthwise, with right sides together. Sew lengthwise along raw edge with Running Stitch. Begin with 1" width at top and taper to ¾", leaving open where marked.

16 Turn right side out. Stuff firmly with polyester stuffing.

17 Fold small end of each leg in ¼" and sew around bottom with Gather Stitch. Pull gather to close and shape feet. Knot to secure.

18 Sew legs to body with Ladder Stitch.

Mane & Tail

19 Measure from back of head to bottom of neck and add an extra 1" for tassel at end of tail.

20 Using fabric scissors, cut measured length from sock as shown in Diagram C.

21 Using fabric scissors, cut ¼"-wide slants to within ¼" of fold along length as shown in Diagram C. Cut 1" off end of mane for tail tassel.

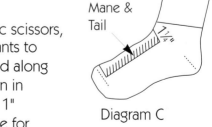

Mane & Tail

Diagram C

22 Sew mane to center of neck with Ladder

Stitch. Begin at base of neck and end at back of head, then back down to base of neck.

23 Turn tail piece, with right sides together. Sew raw edge with Running Stitch, leaving open where marked.

24 Turn right side out. Stuff with polyester stuffing.

25 Using fabric scissors, cut ¼" off tip of tail. Fold tassel in half and poke ends into tip of tail. Sew around tip of tail with Running Stitch to secure tassel to tail.

26 Sew tail to body with Ladder Stitch.

Antlers

27 Cut two ¾" x 1½" pieces from tan sock. Roll each piece lengthwise into a tube-shape. Tuck one end of each piece under ¼".

28 Sew lengthwise along raw edge, with Running Stitch. Sew around tucked end ¼" from top with Gather Stitch. Pull gather snugly, forming knob. Knot to secure.

29 Sew antlers to head in front of ears with Ladder Stitch.

Finish

30 Using fabric scissors, cut 1"-wide strip from cuff of red sock. Fold outer edges to center. Place strip around base of neck. Sew collar in place with Running Stitch.

31 Using small paintbrush, brush blush lightly on cheeks.

George Giraffe

(Pictured at right on page 27.)
Materials & Tools on page 13
Blush

Button: miniature
Felt: brown, red (scraps)
Socks: 1 pair, crew, gold, for body; 1 sock, crew, tan, for mane and antlers

Instructions

Assemble George Giraffe according to Giraffe's instructions and the additional instructions listed below.

Finish

1 Measure neck circumference. Using fabric scissors, cut brown felt 2"-wide and length of neck circumference.

2 Wrap felt rectangle around neck. Tack ends together in front and fold top down for collar.

3 Using fabric scissors, cut ¾" x 1¾" rectangle from red felt. Gather rectangle in center and tack to form bow tie.

Moose 💜

Materials & Tools on page 13

Embroidery floss: brown

Socks: 1 pair, crew, dk. brown, for body; 1 pair, crew, cream, for antlers; 1 sock, crew, red, for tie

Instructions

1 Begin by reading General Instructions on pages 5–13. Stitches and special techniques used are explained in the General Instructions.

2 Organize all materials and tools needed for project. Using fabric marker, mark cutting lines onto socks as shown in Diagrams A-D.

3 Using fabric scissors, cut out marked pieces from socks.

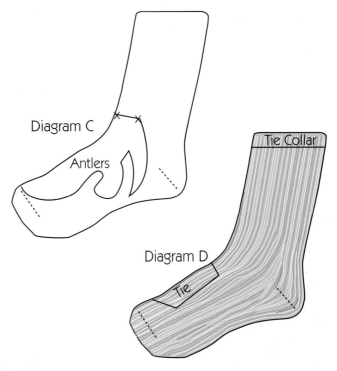

Diagram C

Antlers

Tie Collar

Diagram D

Tie

Note: Ear pieces are 2½" square.

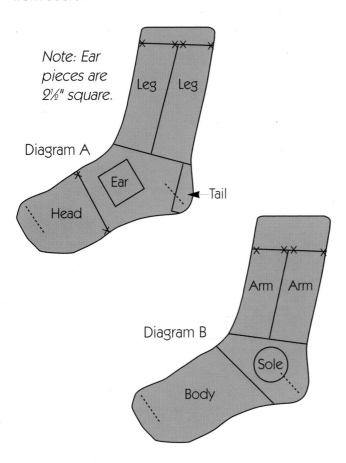

Diagram A

Leg Leg

Ear

Head

Tail

Diagram B

Arm Arm

Sole

Body

Head & Face

4 Stuff head piece firmly with polyester stuffing, with toe seam down for mouth.

5 Sculpt eye area of face. Attach safety eyes to sculpted area.

6 Sew around opening with Gather Stitch. Pull gather to close. Knot to secure.

7 Sew 3" line across face, from side to side, underneath eyes with tight Running Stitch, forming nose.

8 Sculpt nose area of face with embroidery floss.

Ears

9 Fold each ear piece in half, with right sides together. Using fabric marker and fabric scissors, mark and cut out as shown in Diagram E.

Fold

Diagram E

10 With ear pieces still folded, sew along raw edge of each ear with Running Stitch, leaving curved bottom end open where marked as shown in Diagram E.

11 Sew a dart as shown in Diagram F on opposite side of seam with Running Stitch.

12 Turn right side out. Sew to sides of head with Ladder Stitch. Dart should face forward.

Diagram F

Body

13 Stuff body firmly with polyester stuffing.

14 Sew opening closed with Ladder Stitch. Sew head to body with Ladder Stitch.

Arms & Legs

15 Fold each arm and leg piece lengthwise, with right sides together. Sew lengthwise along raw edge of each arm and leg with Running Stitch, leaving open where marked.

16 Place a sole piece inside end of each leg, with right sides together. Sew around edges tightly with Ladder Stitch.

17 Sew a "V"-shape hoof in one end of each arm with Running Stitch. Using fabric scissors, cut away excess sock from "V"-shape.

18 Turn right side out. Stuff to within 1" of open ends with polyester stuffing.

19 Sew arms and legs to body with Ladder Stitch.

Antlers

20 Fold antler piece, with right sides together. Sew raw edges of each antler with Running Stitch, leaving open where marked.

21 Turn right side out. Stuff with polyester stuffing.

22 Sew antlers to head with Ladder Stitch. *Note: Moose's antlers have been tacked down behind the ears for a more realistic look. Experiment for desired look.*

Tail

23 Roll tail piece lengthwise into a tube-shape. Sew lengthwise with Running Stitch. Tie piece of thread ¼" from one end of tube. Pull thread tight. Knot to secure.

24 Fray end of tail ¼".

25 Sew tail to body with Ladder Stitch. Fold end of tail up and tack to secure.

Tie

26 Fold outer edges of tie collar to center. Place collar around neck.

27 Fold top outer edges of tie in ½" and sew in place with Running Stitch. Sew across top of tie with Gather Stitch. Pull slightly to gather. Knot to secure.

28 Tuck gathered end of tie under collar. Tack to secure.

On the Farm

Rabbit 💜

Materials & Tools on page 13
Blush

Socks: 1 sock, crew, lt. green, for carrot top; 1 pair, crew, multicolor, for shirt; 1 sock, crew, orange, for carrot; 1 sock, crew, pink, for overalls; 1 pair, crew, white, for feet, head, and hands

Instructions

1 Begin by reading General Instructions on pages 5–13. Stitches and special techniques used are explained in the General Instructions.

2 Organize all materials and tools needed for project. Using fabric marker, mark cutting lines onto socks as shown in Diagrams A–F.

3 Using fabric scissors, cut out marked pieces from socks.

Head & Ears

4 Fold head piece, with right sides together and heel facing up. Heel is face.

5 From toe end of sock with heel facing up, sew ear shape down 5½", four stitches across, and up 5½" with Running Stitch as shown in Diagram G. Using fabric scissors, cut between ear seams to remove excess sock.

6 Turn right side out. Stuff head firmly with polyester stuffing.

7 Sculpt eyes, nose, and mouth area of face. Attach safety eyes to sculpted area.

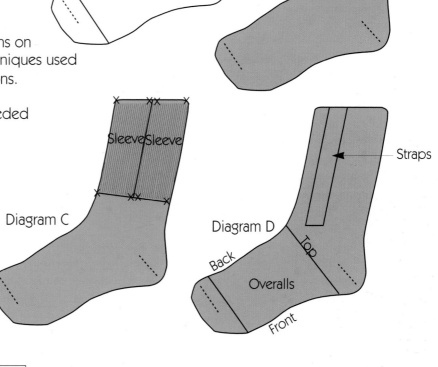

Note: Cut each foot and hand piece on fold, creating four pieces of each.

Foot
Foot
Hand Hand

Diagram A

Head & Ears

Shirt

Diagram

Sleeve Sleeve

Diagram C

Straps

Diagram D

Top
Back
Overalls
Front

Diagram G

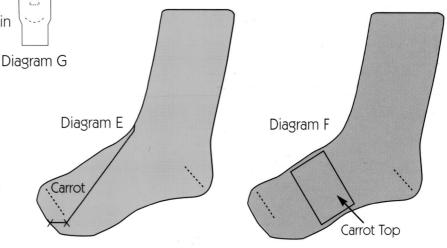

Diagram E

Carrot

Diagram F

Carrot Top

8 Sew around opening of head with Gather Stitch. Pull tightly to close. Knot to secure.

9 Sew around bottom of ears with Gather Stitch. Pull gather slightly to shape. Tack bottom sides of ears together.

Hands

10 Fold hand pieces, with right sides together. Sew along raw edge with Running Stitch, leaving open where marked.

11 Turn right side out. Stuff with polyester stuffing.

12 Sew across openings with Running Stitch.

Feet

13 Fold foot pieces, with right sides together. Sew lengthwise along raw edge with Running Stitch, leaving open where marked.

14 Turn right side out. Stuff with polyester stuffing.

15 Sew across openings with Running Stitch. Sew end of each foot with a long Loop Stitch for toe. Repeat to form four toes on each foot.

Shirt

16 Sew along raw edge of shirt with Gather Stitch. Pull gather to close. Knot to secure.

17 Stuff firmly with polyester stuffing.

18 Sew across open end of shirt with Running Stitch. Sew head to gathered end of shirt body with Ladder Stitch.

Sleeves

19 Fold each sleeve piece lengthwise, with right sides together. Sew lengthwise along raw edge with Running Stitch, leaving open where marked.

20 Turn right side out. Place a hand in end of each sleeve. Sew hands to sleeves with Gather Stitch ¼" from raw edge of sleeves. Pull snugly to gather. Knot to secure.

21 Stuff sleeve with polyester stuffing.

22 Sew sleeves to shirt with Ladder Stitch.

Overalls

23 Using fabric scissors, cut overall piece as shown in Diagram H, forming overall bib.

Diagram H

24 Turn top raw edge in ¼" and sew around one edge of overalls with Running Stitch.

25 Pull overalls over shirt. Top of overalls should be down ¾" from front of neck. Sew Running Stitch all around top edge of overalls to secure to body.

26 Stuff firmly with polyester stuffing.

27 Turn bottom edge of overall leg up and turn again to create ½" cuff. Sew a Running Stitch around edge of cuff to secure to overall leg.

28 Beginning 4" from top center of overalls and ending at bottom of cuffs, sew down center of overalls through front and back with Running Stitch, shaping legs.

29 Place a foot in end of each overall leg. Sew foot to each overall leg with Running Stitch.

30 Fold straps lengthwise, with raw edges to center of straps. Sew along center of straps lengthwise with Running Stitch.

31 Tuck and sew one end of each strap into front of overalls with Running Stitch. See photo on page 34. Place straps over shoulders and cross in back. Tuck and sew ends in back of overalls with Running Stitch.

Carrot

32 Fold carrot piece lengthwise, with right sides together. Sew along raw edge with Running Stitch, leaving open where marked.

33 Turn right side out. Stuff with polyester stuffing.

34 Sew open end closed with Running Stitch.

35 Cut ¼" slits down carrot top piece to within ¼" of bottom edge as shown in Diagram I.

Diagram I

36 Roll bottom edge tightly to the right. Tack in place and sew to top of carrot with Ladder Stitch.

Finish

37 Using small paintbrush, brush blush lightly on cheeks and inside ears.

Mother Rabbit

(Photo on page 38.)
Materials & Tools on page 13
Beaded pins: black head (2); pink head (1)
Blush
Buttons: heart, white, 8 mm (2)
Lace trim: (scraps)
Ribbon: ¼"-wide (scraps)
Socks: 1 sock, crew, blue, for overalls; 1 pair, crew, burgundy, for shirt, bow, and flower; 1 sock, crew (scrap), green, for leaves; 1 pair, crew, white, for feet, head, hands, and baby; 1 sock, crew (scrap), yellow, for flower
Straw hat: 2"-dia.

Instructions

Assemble Mother Rabbit according to Rabbit's instructions, Diagram A for Baby, and the additional instructions below.

1 Adhere piece of lace around neck with craft glue. Sew heart buttons to front of overalls where bottom of straps and top of overalls join.

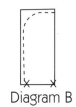

Diagram A

Baby

Ear Ear

2 Using fabric scissors, cut ¾" circle from burgundy sock. Cut ½" circle from scrap of yellow sock. Sew circles together for flower.

3 Using fabric scissors, cut two small leaves from scrap of green sock and sew to bottom of flower. Adhere flower to front center of overalls between heart buttons with craft glue. Make a bow from burgundy sock. Adhere in front of one ear with craft glue.

Baby

4 Fold baby piece, with right sides together. Sew along raw edge with Running Stitch as shown in Diagram B, leaving open where marked. Using fabric scissors, cut away excess sock.

Diagram B

5 Turn right side out. Stuff with polyester stuffing.

6 Sew across open edge with Gather Stitch. Pull gather closed. Knot to secure.

7 Fold each ear piece lengthwise, with right sides together. Sew lengthwise along raw edge with Running Stitch as shown in Diagram C. Using fabric scissors, cut away excess sock.

Diagram C

8 Turn right side out. Adhere to back of head with craft glue.

9 Tie 3" piece of carpet thread tight around neck to define head. Knot to secure.

10 Wrap ribbon strip around neck and tie into a bow.

11 Using wire cutters, cut off pins to within ¼" of head. Dip cut pin end in craft glue and push into face for eyes and nose.

12 Using small paintbrush, brush blush lightly on cheeks and inside ears.

13 Place straw hat on baby's head. Tuck ears inside of hat. Adhere baby to rabbit's arm with craft glue.

Frog ♥

(Photo on page 39.)
Materials & Tools on page 13
Blush
Felt: black (scrap)
Socks: 1 pair, crew, green and yellow tie-dyed,
   for body; 1 sock, crew, purple, for bow tie

Instructions

1 Begin by reading General Instructions on pages 5–13. Stitches and special techniques used are explained in the General Instructions.

2 Organize all materials and tools needed for project. Using fabric marker, mark cutting lines onto socks as shown in Diagrams A–B.

3 Using fabric scissors, cut out marked pieces from socks.

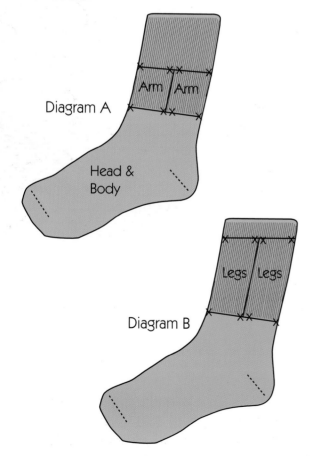

Diagram A

Arm | Arm

Head & Body

Diagram B

Legs | Legs

Head

4 Stuff toe area of body piece firmly with polyester stuffing. Toe seam is mouth.

5 Sew circle slightly off center top of head with Gather Stitch. Pull gather slightly, creating a bulge as shown in Diagram C.

Diagram C

6 Stuff bulge with polyester stuffing.

7 Pull bulge snug, and knot to secure. Repeat process to create second bulge. Using fabric scissors, cut small felt circles for eyes. Sew felt eyes to bulged areas.

8 Stuff head firmly with polyester stuffing. Head should measure approximately 4" from top to bottom.

9 Measure down 2⅜" from center of mouth and sew across sock through front and back with Running Stitch, curving at ends as shown in Diagram D, forming head.

Diagram D

Body

10 Stuff remaining 3½" of body piece with polyester stuffing.

11 Sew curved line across bottom of sock with Running Stitch, forming bottom of body. Sew over Running Stitch with Ladder Stitch.

Arms & Legs

12 Fold arm and leg pieces lengthwise, with right sides together. Sew lengthwise along raw edge with Running Stitch, leaving open where marked.

13 Sew three toes or fingers on one end of each leg or arm with Running Stitch as shown in Diagram E. Using fabric scissors, cut away excess sock between toes.

Diagram E

14 Turn right side out. Stuff with polyester stuffing.

15 Sew in between each finger and toe with a continuous long Loop Stitch.

16 Sew across each arm and leg (1" from end of toes or fingers) with Running Stitch to shape hands and feet as shown in Diagram F.

Diagram F

17 Sew arms and legs to body with Ladder Stitch.

Finish

18 Using fabric scissors, cut 1" strip from foot of purple sock. Gather center and tack, forming a bow tie. Tack to body.

19 Using small paintbrush, brush blush lightly on cheeks and mouth.

Frederick Frog

Materials & Tools on page 13
Blush
Socks: 1 pair, crew, green, for body; 1 sock, crew, red, for bow tie

Instructions
Assemble Frederick Frog according to Frog instructions and the additional instructions below.

Bow Tie

1 Using fabric scissors, cut 1" strip from foot of red sock. Gather center and tack, forming a bow tie. Tack to body.

Note: Frederick Frog has been embellished with a flower, a fly on a wire, and has been placed on a park bench, with stepping stones leading to his gold fish pond for a more elaborate setting.

Chicken ♥

Materials & Tools on page 13

Blush

Socks: 1 sock, crew, gold, for beak, feet and legs;
1 sock, crew, red, for comb, and wattle; 1 pair,
men's, crew, white, terry, for body, tail, and
wings

Instructions

1 Begin by reading General Instructions on pages
5–13. Stitches and special techniques used are
explained in the General Instructions.

2 Organize all materials and tools needed for
project. *Note: Turn men's white terry crew socks,
so looped side becomes right side.* Using fabric
marker, mark cutting lines onto socks as shown in
Diagrams A-D.

3 Using fabric scissors, cut out marked pieces
from socks.

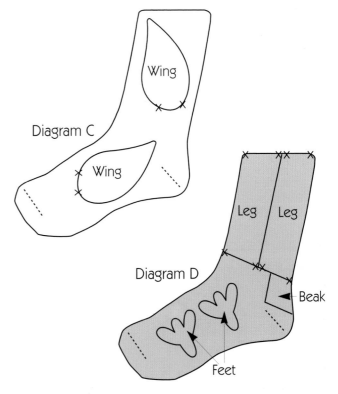

Diagram C

Diagram D

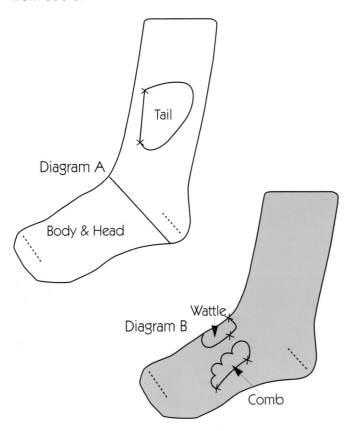

Diagram A

Diagram B

Head & Body

4 Turn body and head piece wrong side out with
toe seam facing up.

5 Sew head and body piece along each
side with Running Stitch as shown in
Diagram E, leaving top open. Using
fabric scissors, cut away excess sock.

Diagram E

6 Turn right side out. Seam will be in
center front and back of chicken head.

7 Attach safety eyes to face.

8 Stuff firmly with polyester stuffing.

9 Sew opening closed with Straight Stitch.

Wings

10 Place wing pieces, with right sides together.
Sew around each wing with Running Stitch,
leaving open where marked.

11 Turn right side out. Stuff lightly with polyester stuffing.

12 Sew each wing opening closed with Straight Stitch.

13 Sew through each wing with tight Running Stitch to define feathered features as shown in Diagram F.

Diagram F

14 Sew pointed tip of wings to body with Ladder Stitch.

Tail

15 Place tail pieces, with right sides together. Sew along raw edges with Running Stitch, leaving open where marked.

16 Turn right side out. Stuff lightly with polyester stuffing.

17 Sew tail opening closed with Running Stitch.

18 Sew through tail with Running Stitch, forming feathered features. Repeat stitching back and forth until feathered features are defined as shown in Diagram G.

Diagram G

19 Sew tail vertically to back of body with Ladder Stitch.

Beak

20 Fold beak piece in half, with right sides together. Sew edge as shown in Diagram H, leaving open where marked. Using fabric scissors, cut away excess sock.

Diagram H

21 Turn right side out. Stuff with polyester stuffing.

22 Sew beak to face with Ladder Stitch, seam down.

Wattle & Comb

23 Fold wattle piece in half widthwise, with right sides together. Sew along raw edge with Running Stitch, leaving open where marked.

24 Turn right side out. Stuff with polyester stuffing.

25 Sew wattle under beak with Ladder Stitch, seam down.

26 Fold comb pieces, with right sides together. Sew scalloped edge with Running Stitch, leaving open where marked.

27 Turn right side out. Stuff lightly with polyester stuffing.

28 Sew opening closed with Running Stitch.

29 Sew comb to top center of head with Ladder Stitch.

Feet & Legs

30 Fold leg pieces lengthwise, with right sides together. Sew lengthwise along raw edge with Running Stitch.

31 Turn right side out. Stuff in middle to shape calves with polyester stuffing, leaving ends unstuffed.

32 Place foot pieces, with right sides together. Sew along raw edges with Running Stitch. Cut a slit in top of each foot to turn.

33 Turn right side out. Stuff with polyester stuffing.

34 Sew slit closed with Ladder Stitch. Sew feet to legs on top of slit with Ladder Stitch. Sew legs to body with Ladder Stitch.

Finish

35 Using small paintbrush, brush blush lightly on cheeks.

Dog

(Photo on page 45.)
Materials & Tools on page 13
Blush
Fabric: 7" square
Socks: 1 pair, crew, med. gray, for body and outer ears; 1 sock, crew, lt. gray, for inner ears

Instructions

1 Begin by reading General Instructions on pages 5–13. Stitches and special techniques used are explained in the General Instructions.

2 Organize all materials and tools needed for project. Using fabric marker, mark cutting lines onto socks as shown in Diagrams A–C.

3 Using fabric scissors, cut out marked pieces from socks.

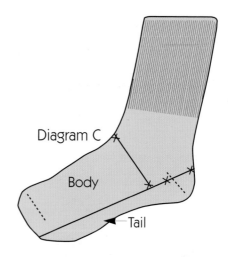

Diagram C

Body

Tail

Head

4 Fold head piece, with right sides together. Toe seam is mouth. Sew head piece with Running Stitch as shown in Diagram D, leaving open where marked. Using fabric scissors, cut away excess sock.

Diagram D

5 Turn right side out. Stuff firmly with polyester stuffing.

6 Sculpt eye area of face. Attach safety eyes to sculpted area. Attach safety nose to face.

7 Sew around opening with Gather Stitch. Pull gather to close. Knot to secure.

Body

8 Fold body lengthwise, with right sides together. Sew lengthwise along raw edge with Running Stitch, leaving open where marked.

9 Turn right side out. Stuff firmly with polyester stuffing.

10 Sew around opening with Gather Stitch. Pull gather to close. Knot to secure.

11 Sew gathered end of head to body with Ladder Stitch. Toe seam is facing up.

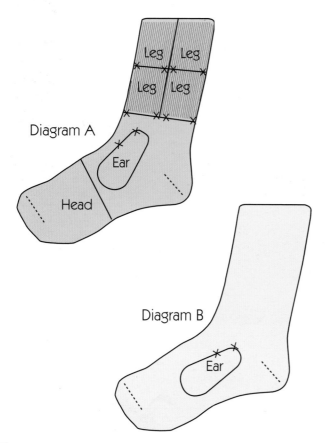

Leg Leg
Leg Leg

Diagram A

Ear

Head

Diagram B

Ear

Tail

12 Fold tail piece lengthwise, with right sides together. Sew lengthwise along raw edge with Running Stitch, tapering toward end of tail, leaving open where marked.

13 Turn right side out. Sew wider end of tail to end of body with Ladder Stitch.

Legs

14 Fold each leg piece lengthwise, with right sides together. Sew lengthwise along raw edge and across one end with Running Stitch, leaving open where marked.

15 Turn right side out. Stuff firmly with polyester stuffing.

16 Sew legs to body with Ladder Stitch.

17 Sew three toes on each foot with Loop Stitch.

Ears

18 Place one dark ear piece and one light ear piece, with right sides together. Sew along raw edge with Running Stitch, leaving open where marked. Repeat for remaining ear pieces.

19 Turn right side out. Turn open ends in ¼" and sew closed with Ladder Stitch. Sew small curved end of ears to head with Ladder Stitch. Inner ear should face down.

Finish

20 Using small paintbrush, brush blush lightly onto cheeks and mouth.

21 Fold fabric square into a triangle. Tie triangle around neck and tack to body for kerchief.

Rolph

(Pictured at right on page 45.)

Materials & Tools on page 13
Blush
Chain: 6"
Jump ring: (size will depend on size of chain links)
Socks: 1 pair, crew, tan, for body; 1 sock, crew, contrasting brown, for inner ears

Instructions

Assemble Rolph according to Dog's instructions and the additional instructions below.

1 Place 6" chain around neck and attach ends together with a jump ring, for chain collar.

Pig

Materials & Tools on page 13
Fabric: 1"-wide (16")
Socks: 1 pair, crew, pink, for body

Instructions

1 Begin by reading General Instructions on pages 5–13. Stitches and special techniques used are explained in the General Instructions.

2 Organize all materials and tools needed for project. Using fabric marker, mark cutting lines onto socks as shown in Diagrams A–B.

3 Using fabric scissors, cut out marked pieces from socks.

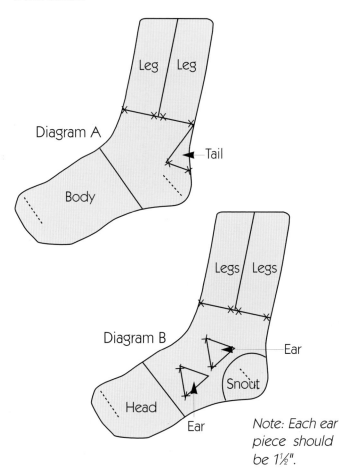

Diagram A

Diagram B

Note: Each ear piece should be 1½".

Head

4 Stuff firmly with polyester stuffing.

5 Sculpt eye area of face. Attach safety eyes.

6 Sew around opening with Gather Stitch. Pull gather to close. Knot to secure.

Snout

7 Stuff firmly with polyester stuffing.

8 Sew along raw edge with Gather Stitch. Pull gather slightly to shape snout. Sew snout to head with Ladder Stitch.

Body

9 Stuff firmly with polyester stuffing.

10 Sew around opening with Gather Stitch. Pull gather to close. Knot to secure. Sew head to body with Ladder Stitch.

11 Using 5" doll needle, sculpt snout area of face, going through head and neck for nostrils. Attach small safety eyes for nostrils.

12 Using 3" doll needle, sew head to body with Ladder Stitch.

Ears

13 Place two ear pieces, with right sides together. Sew along raw edges of two sides with Running Stitch, leaving open where marked. Repeat for second ear.

14 Turn right side out. Sew ears to head with Ladder Stitch.

15 Sew a small stitch in tip of each ear and pull forward to shape a flap.

Legs

16 Fold legs lengthwise, with right sides together. Sew lengthwise along raw edge with Running Stitch, leaving open where marked.

17 Sew "V"-shape hoof in one end of each leg with Running Stitch. Using fabric scissors, trim away excess fabric.

18 Turn right side out. Stuff with polyester stuffing.

19 Sew legs to body with Ladder Stitch.

20 Sew center of each hoof with a long Loop Stitch.

Tail

21 Fold tail lengthwise, with right sides together. Sew lengthwise along diagonal with Running Stitch, leaving open where marked.

22 Turn right side out. Sew open end of tail to back of body with Ladder Stitch.

23 Sew along top of tail with Gather Stitch. Pull gather to shape curled tail. Knot to secure.

Finish

24 Place fabric strip around neck and tie into a bow.

25 Using small paintbrush, brush blush lightly onto cheeks and inside ears.

Percival

Materials & Tools on page 13
Beads: black (2)
Fabric: 7" square; ¼"-wide (7")
Silverware
Socks: 1 pair, crew, pink, for body
Straw hat: 4"-dia.

Instructions
Assemble Percival according to Pig's instructions and the additional instructions below.

1 Adhere a bead to each nostril indentation with craft glue.

2 Using fabric scissors, cut 7" strip from fabric. Adhere fabric strip around brim of straw hat with craft glue. Adhere hat to head with craft glue.

3 Fold fabric square into a triangle and tie around neck.

4 Tack a fork in one hand and a spoon in another.

Note: Percival has been surrounded by plastic fruits and vegetables, and placed in a hammock for a more elaborate setting.

Bee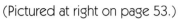

(Pictured at right on page 53.)

Materials & Tools on page 13

Blush

Embroidered floss: black

Felt: black (scrap)

Socks: 3 socks, crew, black, for arms, hat, legs, and stripes; 1 sock, crew, red, for collar; 1 pair, crew, white, for wings; 1 sock, crew, yellow, for body and head

Instructions

1 Begin by reading General Instructions on pages 5–13. Stitches and special techniques used are explained in the General Instructions.

2 Organize all materials and tools needed for project. Using fabric marker, mark cutting lines onto socks as shown in Diagrams A–D.

3 Using fabric scissors, cut out marked pieces from socks.

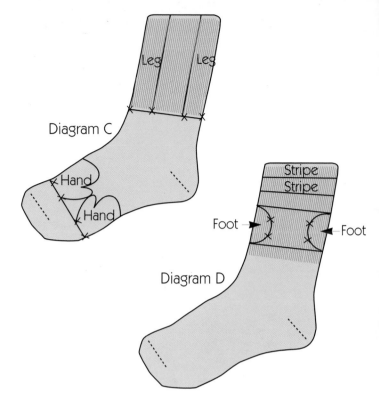

Diagram C

Diagram D

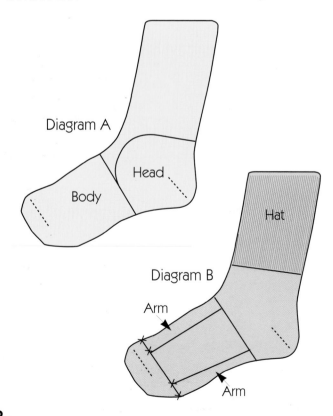

Diagram A

Diagram B

Head

4 Sew around opening with Gather Stitch. Pull gather slightly, leave unsecured.

5 Stuff head piece firmly with polyester stuffing. Head is larger than body.

6 Sculpt eye area of face. Using fabric scissors, cut small felt circles for eyes and nose. Sew felt eyes to sculpted area.

7 Sew felt nose to face. Embroider mouth onto face. Pull gather to close. Knot to secure.

Body

8 Stuff body piece lightly with polyester stuffing. Body should be slender.

9 Sew around opening with Gather Stitch. Pull gather to close. Knot to secure.

Continued on page 54.

Continued from page 52.

Arms & Hands

10 Fold each arm piece lengthwise, with right sides together. Sew lengthwise along raw edges with Running Stitch, leaving open where marked.

11 Fold each hand piece, with right sides together. Sew along raw edges with Running Stitch, leaving open where marked.

12 Turn arms and hands right side out.

13 Sew across opening of hand with Running Stitch.

14 Place a hand in end of each arm. Sew hand to arm with Running Stitch. Turn other end of each arm in ¼". Sew arms to body with Ladder Stitch.

Legs & Feet

15 Fold each leg piece lengthwise, with right sides together. Sew lengthwise along raw edges with Running Stitch, leaving open where marked.

16 Place foot pieces, with right sides together. Sew along curved edges with Running Stitch, leaving open where marked.

17 Turn legs and feet right side out. Stuff feet firmly with polyester stuffing.

18 Place a leg in open end of each foot. Sew foot to leg with Running Stitch. Turn other end of each leg in ¼". Sew legs to body with Ladder Stitch.

Hat & Antennae

19 Turn hat piece wrong side out.

20 Beginning at raw edge of cuff, sew up 3½", then four stitches across, and down 3½" with Running Stitch as shown in Diagram E, forming antennae. Cut between antennae seams.

Diagram E

21 Turn right side out.

22 Fold each antenna lengthwise, with outer edges to the center, and fold again. Beginning at top and ending at base of antenna, sew folded edges together with Gather Stitch. Pull gather snugly to shape curved antennae. Knot to secure.

23 Place hat on head and turn edge up 1½" for cuff.

24 Sew hat to head with Running Stitch.

Stripes

25 Fold outer edges to center. Place each stripe around body. Sew stripes to body with Running Stitch.

Finish

26 Using fabric scissors, cut 1"-wide strip from cuff of red sock. Fold outer edges to center. Place collar around neck. Sew collar to neck and body with Running Stitch.

27 Using small paintbrush, brush blush lightly onto cheeks.

28 See Wings on page 95. Make wings.

29 Sew wings to back of bee with Ladder Sttich.

Beesley

(Pictured at left on page 53.)
Materials & Tools on page 13
Blush
Craft glue
Socks: 3 socks, crew, black, for arms, hat, legs, and stripes; 1 sock, crew, red, for collar; 1 pair, crew, white for wings; 1 sock, crew, yellow, for body and head
Wire: 19-gauge, black

Instructions

Assemble Beesley Bee according to Bee's instructions and the additional instructions below.

Face

1 Using wire cutters, cut off shank from safety eyes and nose. Adhere eyes and nose to face with craft glue.

2 Using needle nose pliers, shape mouth from black wire. Bend ends of mouth. Dip ends in craft glue. Push into face.

3 Cut 1½" x 2" strip from red sock. Fold strip in half widthwise, with right sides together. Sew lengthwise along raw edge and across one end.

4 Turn right side out. Sew open end closed with Ladder Stitch. Gather center of strip and tack to neck, for bow tie.

Moonique

(Photo on page 56.)
Materials & Tools on page 13
Blush
Cowbells: 9 mm, gold (2)
Fabric: 1"-wide (26")
Felt: black (scrap)
Socks: 1 pair, crew, black, for body, outer ears, head, and legs; 1 sock, crew, white, for hooves, inner ears, muzzle, and tail

Instructions

1 Begin by reading General Instructions on pages 5–13. Stitches and special techniques used are explained in the General Instructions.

2 Organize all materials and tools needed for project. Using fabric marker, mark cutting lines onto socks as shown in Diagrams A–C.

3 Using fabric scissors, cut out marked pieces from socks.

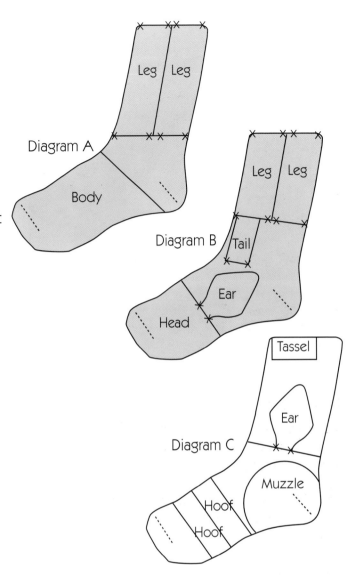

Body

4 Stuff body firmly with polyester stuffing.

5 Sew around opening with Gather Stitch. Pull gather to close. Knot to secure.

Head

6 Stuff head firmly with polyester stuffing to measure 3½" in diameter.

7 Sculpt eye area of face. Attach eyes to sculpted area.
Continued on page 57.

Moonique • Moonique • Moonique • Moonique • Moonique
CREAM
COWA
BUNGA
COOKIES
MORE CHIPS

Continued from page 55.

8 Sew around opening with Gather Stitch. Pull gather to close. Knot to secure.

9 Sew head to body with Ladder Stitch.

Muzzle

10 Sew around raw edge with Gather Stitch. Pull slightly to gather, leaving unsecured.

11 Stuff with polyester stuffing.

12 Pull gather to desired shape. Knot to secure.

13 Sew muzzle to face with Ladder Stitch.

14 Using 5" doll needle, sculpt nose, going through muzzle, head, and neck.

15 Using fabric scissors, cut two small felt circles for nostrils. Sew felt nostrils to sculpted area.

Ears

16 Place one dark ear piece and one light ear piece, with right sides together. Using 3" doll needle, sew along raw edge with Running Stitch, leaving open where marked. Repeat for remaining ear pieces.

17 Turn right side out. Sew across open ends with Gather Stitch. Pull snugly to gather. Knot to secure.

18 Sew gathered end of ears to head with Ladder Stitch. Inner ear should face forward.

Legs & Hooves

19 Turn one hoof piece and one leg piece, with right sides together. Sew across bottom raw edge with Running Stitch as shown in Diagram D. Finger-press seam and open so white piece

Diagram D

is at bottom of leg. Repeat for other three legs and hooves.

20 Fold each leg lengthwise, with right sides together. Sew lengthwise along raw edge of each leg with Running Stitch.

21 Sew "V"-shape in each hoof with Running Stitch. Using fabric scissors, trim away excess sock.

22 Turn right side out. Stuff to within 1" of open end. Leg should appear as shown in Diagram E.

Diagram E

23 Sew 5" legs to bottom of body and 4" legs to top of body with Ladder Stitch.

Tail

24 Fold tail lengthwise, with right sides together. Sew lengthwise along raw edge with Running Stitch, leaving open where marked.

25 Turn right side out. Sew around one end of tail with Gather Stitch, leaving unsecured.

26 Cut slits in tassel piece to ¼" from top edge as shown in Diagram F. Roll top edge tightly to the right. Tuck into gathered tip of tail. Pull tail gathers snugly to gather around tassel. Knot to secure.

Diagram F

27 Sew tassel to tail with Running Stitch.

28 Sew tail to body with Ladder Stitch.

Finish

28 Using small paintbrush, brush blush lightly on inside ears and muzzle.

29 Sew cowbell to bottom of each ear for earring.

30 Wrap fabric strip around neck. Tie into a bow.

At a Party

  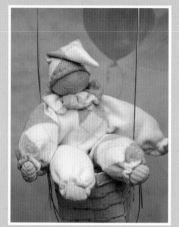 

Angel 🤍

(Photo on page 59.)

Materials & Tools on page 13

Blush

Embroidery yarn

Satin ribbon: ⅛"-wide, mauve (12")

Socks: 1 pair, knee-highs, mauve, for dress; 1 pair, crew, white, for body, hands, and head; 1 pair, crew, white, for wings

Instructions

1 Begin by reading General Instructions on pages 5–13. Stitches and special techniques used are explained in the General Instructions.

2 Organize all materials and tools needed for project. Using fabric marker, mark cutting lines onto socks as shown in Diagrams A–C.

3 Using fabric scissors, cut out marked pieces from socks. Head and body are one piece.

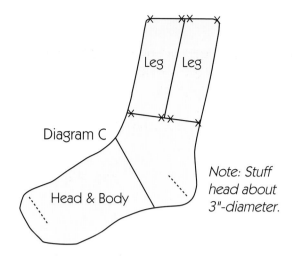

Diagram C

Head & Body

Leg   Leg

Note: Stuff head about 3"-diameter.

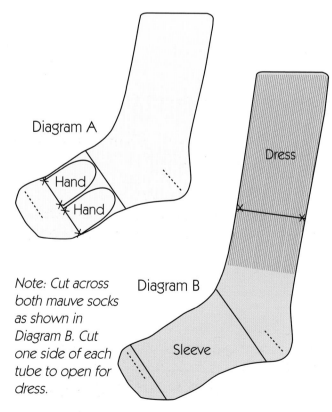

Diagram A

Hand

Hand

Dress

Diagram B

Sleeve

Note: Cut across both mauve socks as shown in Diagram B. Cut one side of each tube to open for dress.

Head & Body

4 Stuff toe firmly with polyester stuffing, forming head.

5 Sew around bottom of head with Gather Stitch. Pull gather slightly, leaving unsecured, forming neck.

6 Create eyes with French Knot. Pull gather snugly. Knot to secure.

7 Stuff body firmly with polyester stuffing.

8 Sew across raw edges with Running Stitch. Sew over Running Stitch with Ladder Stitch.

9 Sew around bottom of head and top of body with Ladder Stitch for stability.

Legs

10 Fold leg pieces lengthwise, with right sides together. Sew lengthwise along raw edge of each leg with Running Stitch, leaving open where marked. Sew across one end of each leg with Running Stitch, curving to form foot.

11 Turn right side out. Stuff with polyester stuffing.

12 Sew legs to body with Ladder Stitch.

Hands

13 Place hand pieces, with right sides together. Sew along curved edge with Running Stitch, leaving open where marked.

14 Turn right side out. Stuff with polyester stuffing.

15 Sew across open ends with Running Stitch.

Dress

16 Place dress pieces, with right sides together. Sew lengthwise along raw edges with Running Stitch, leaving open where marked.

17 Turn one raw edge down ¼" and sew with Gather Stitch, leaving unsecured. This is top of dress.

18 Place dress on body. Pull thread to gather snugly at neck. Knot to secure.

19 Turn bottom of dress up ½" and sew around bottom with Running Stitch.

20 Using ruler, measure six even points around bottom. Sew 1" from bottom of each point with Gather Stitch. Pull each gather snugly. Knot to secure, making scalloped edge.

Sleeves

21 Turn up ½" on one end. Sew around with Gather Stitch, leaving unsecured.

22 Place a hand in end of each cuff. Pull tightly. Sew hand to cuff with Running Stitch.

23 Sew top of sleeves with Gather Stitch. Pull thread to gather half-closed. Knot to secure.

24 Sew sleeves to dress and body with Ladder Stitch.

Hair

25 Using craft scissors, cut 2" x 4" piece of cardboard.

26 Wrap yarn 18 times around 2" width of cardboard. Gather top with a piece of yarn and tie tight. Slip off end of cardboard. Repeat for 24 bundles.

27 Sew eight bundles across back of head. Sew eight bundles along both sides and across top. Sew remaining eight bundles in center of head.

28 Sew satin ribbon bow to top left side of head.

Finish

29 Using small paintbrush, brush blush lightly onto cheeks.

30 See Wings instructions on page 95. Make wings. Tack wings to back of angel.

Angelina

(Photo on page 62.)
Materials & Tools on page 13
Blush
Buttons: 8 mm, gold (4); 12 mm, pearlescent (2)
Dried flowers: assorted, small
Fabric stiffener
Pineapple doilies: 10"-dia. (2)
Socks: 2 pairs, knee-highs, lavender with silver stripes, for dress; 1 pair, crew, white, for body, hands, and head
Spanish moss: small bag
Wire: 19-gauge, gold

Instructions

Assemble Angelina according to Angel's instructions and the additional instructions below. Sculpt Angelina's face after completing

step #5 on page 60. *Note: Angelina's dress and sleeves are not the same as Angel's. See Diagrams A-B on facing page.*

Dress

1 See "Dress" instructions on page 61. Sew dress pieces together, remembering that three pieces will be sewn together.

Sleeves

2 Fold each sleeve piece lengthwise, with right sides together. Sew lengthwise along raw edge of each sleeve with Running Stitch. Turn right side out.

3 Fold cuff pieces in half, with right sides together. Sew widthwise along raw edges with Running Stitch. Turn right side out.

4 Sew around one end of each sleeve with Gather Stitch. Adjust gather to fit raw edge of each cuff. Knot to secure.

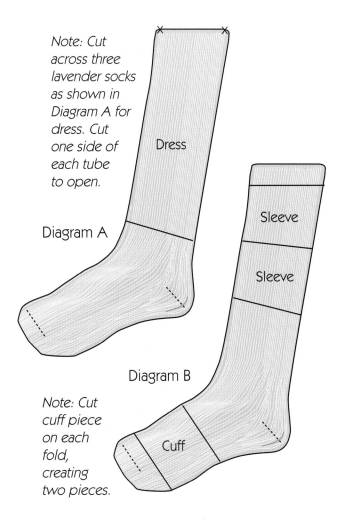

Note: Cut across three lavender socks as shown in Diagram A for dress. Cut one side of each tube to open.

Dress

Diagram A

Sleeve

Sleeve

Diagram B

Note: Cut cuff piece on each fold, creating two pieces.

Cuff

5 Align sleeve and cuff seams, with right sides together. Sew along raw edges of each sleeve and cuff with Running Stitch, attaching sleeve to cuff. Turn end of cuff in ½". Sew around with Running Stitch.

6 Place a hand in end of each cuff. Sew each hand to cuff with Running Stitch.

7 Sew top of sleeves with Gather Stitch, leaving unsecured.

8 Stuff sleeve lightly with polyester stuffing.

9 Pull thread to gather half-closed. Knot to secure. Sew sleeves to dress and body with Ladder Stitch.

Hair & Halo

10 Adhere Spanish moss to head for hair with craft glue.

11 Using wire cutters, cut 10" piece of wire. Thread gold star button 3" from end of wire and twist wire to keep button in place.

12 Thread remaining three buttons, 1½" apart, twisting wire to keep each button in place.

13 Shape wire into oval and twist ends together for halo. Apply craft glue to halo. Push halo into hair carefully.

14 Adhere assorted flowers and pearlescent star buttons randomly to hair around halo and sides of head with craft glue.

Finish

15 Using fabric stiffener, apply to two 10" doilies, following manufacturer's instructions. Fold each doily in half. Let dry.

16 Adhere each wing to back of dress, with fold to center of back, with craft glue.

Note: Angelina has been embellished with a lace collar, ribbon, charms, and small heart buttons for a more elaborate look.

Clown ♥

Materials & Tools on page 13

Embroidery floss: blue, pink

Socks: 1 pair, knee-highs, argyle, pastel, for collar, hat, sleeve, and suit; 1 sock, crew, pink, for body; 1 pair, knee-highs, white, for sleeve and suit

Instructions

1 Begin by reading General Instructions on pages 5–13. Stitches and special techniques used are explained in the General Instructions.

2 Organize all materials and tools needed for project. Using fabric marker, mark cutting lines onto socks as shown in Diagrams A-E.

3 Using fabric scissors, cut 2" off cuff top of socks used for clown suit, Diagram B and Diagram D. Cut out marked pieces from socks.

Head & Body

4 Stuff toe of sock firmly with polyester stuffing, creating head 3" in length.

5 Sew around bottom of head with Gather Stitch. Pull gather snugly to shape head. Knot to secure.

6 Stuff body piece firmly with polyester stuffing.

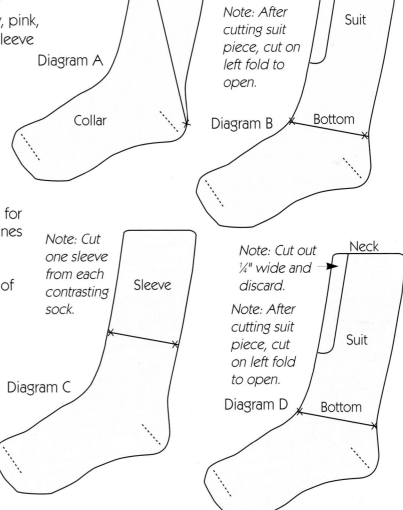

Diagram A — Hat, Collar

Diagram B — *Note: Cut out ¼" wide and discard.* *Note: After cutting suit piece, cut on left fold to open.* — Neck, Suit, Bottom

Diagram C — *Note: Cut one sleeve from each contrasting sock.* — Sleeve

Diagram D — *Note: Cut out ¼" wide and discard.* *Note: After cutting suit piece, cut on left fold to open.* — Neck, Suit, Bottom

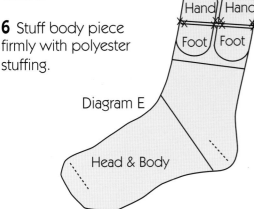

Diagram E — Hand, Hand, Foot, Foot, Head & Body

7 Sew around opening with Gather Stitch. Pull gather to close. Knot to secure.

8 Sew around neck with Ladder Stitch to stabilize head.

Hands & Feet

9 Fold each hand piece, with right sides together. Sew along raw edge with Running Stitch, leaving open where marked.

10 Fold each foot piece, with right sides together. Sew along raw edge with Running Stitch, leaving open where marked.

11 Turn hands and feet right side out. Stuff with polyester stuffing.

12 Sew across openings with Running Stitch.

Suit

13 Place suit pieces with right sides together. Sew curved edges from neck to crotch on each side with Running Stitch.

14 Fold seams with right sides together. Sew up leg to crotch and down to end of leg with Running Stitch.

15 Turn right side out. Stuff with polyester stuffing.

16 Sew around top of suit with Gather Stitch, leaving unsecured. Place suit on body, with top of suit at top of neck. Pull thread to gather snug around neck. Knot to secure.

17 Turn leg end up ½" and sew with Gather Stitch. Place foot in each gathered end of leg. Pull thread to gather snug around each foot. Knot to secure.

18 Sew foot to each leg with Running Stitch.

Sleeves

19 Fold white sleeve piece lengthwise, with right sides together. Sew along raw edge with Running Stitch, leaving open where marked. Repeat for argyle sleeve.

20 Turn right side out. Turn open end of each sleeve in ½". Sew around edge with Gather Stitch, leaving unsecured.

21 Stuff sleeves slightly with polyester stuffing.

22 Place hand in each gathered end of sleeve. Pull thread to gather snug around each hand. Knot to secure.

23 Sew hand to each sleeve with Running Stitch. Sew around open end of sleeve with Gather Stitch. Pull thread, gathering half-closed. Sew sleeves to body with Ladder Stitch.

Collar & Hat

24 Using fabric scissors, cut three 3" x 5" strips from argyle sock. Place strips with right sides together. Sew strips, with right sides together, at 3" edges with Running Stitch, creating collar.

25 Fold sewn strip in half lengthwise, with wrong sides together. Sew along raw edges with Gather Stitch, leaving unsecured. Place collar around neck and pull gather snugly around neck. Knot to secure. (For a double collar, cut strips from white sock following Steps 24–25.)

26 Fold hat piece lengthwise, with right sides together. Sew lengthwise along raw edge with Running Stitch, leaving open where marked.

27 Turn right side out. Turn open end in ¼" and sew to head with Running Stitch.

Finish

28 Using embroidery needle, embroider eyes on face with Cross-stitch.

29 Sew mouth on face with two long Loop Stitches.

Chuckles & Friend

Materials & Tools on page 13
Acrylic button: jeweled
Acrylic jewels: assorted
Socks: 1 pair, knee-highs, pink, for sleeve and suit;
  1 pair, knee-highs, turquoise, for collar, hat,
  sleeve, and suit; 1 sock, crew, white, for body

Instructions
Assemble Chuckles according to Clown's

size small socks.

Finish

1 Adhere acrylic jewels onto face for eyes and nose with craft glue. Adhere acrylic jewels down front of suit with craft glue. See photo above for placement.

2 Sew jeweled button to tip of hat.

Baby Buddies 💗

Materials & Tools on page 13 (for two baby buddies)

Embroidery floss: colors of choice, for eyes and mouth

Socks: 1 pair, crew, color of choice, for head and hands; 2 pairs, crew, contrasting colors of choice, for body, hat, and sweater

Instructions

1 Begin by reading General Instructions on pages 5–13. Stitches and special techniques used are explained in the General Instructions.

2 Organize all materials and tools needed for project. Using fabric marker, mark cutting lines onto socks as shown in Diagrams A–C on page 70.

3 Using fabric scissors, cut out marked pieces from socks. (Body and legs are one piece.)

Body & Legs

4 Fold body piece, with right sides together, with toe seam facing up. Sew up 4" from end of toe, four stitches across, to form crotch, and down other side, with Running Stitch, leaving open where marked as shown in Diagram D.

Diagram D

Sew, rounding ends, forming toes. Using fabric scissors, cut between seams.

5 Turn right side out. Stuff body and legs firmly with polyester stuffing.

6 Sew around opening with Gather Stitch. Pull gather to close. Knot to secure.

7 Sew a Running Stitch across each leg through front and back on toe seam end, forming foot. Sew over Running Stitch with Ladder Stitch, catching edge of toe seam to shape foot.

Head

8 Stuff firmly with polyester stuffing.

9 Sew around opening with Gather Stitch. Pull gather to close. Knot to secure.

10 Sew head to body with Ladder Stitch, placing toe seam on back of head.

11 Using embroidery needle, sew eyes and mouth on face with embroidery floss.

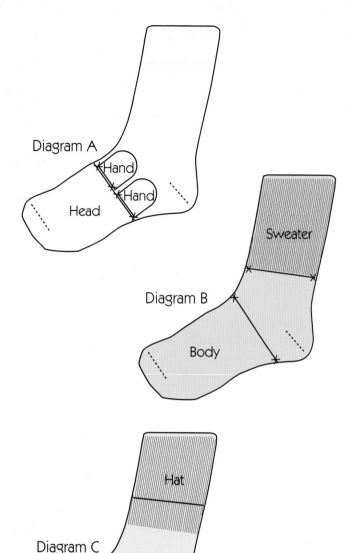

Diagram A

Hand

Hand

Head

Diagram B

Sweater

Body

Diagram C

Hat

Sleeve

Sleeve

14 Sew across open ends with Running Stitch.

Sleeves

15 Fold sleeve pieces lengthwise, with right sides together. Sew lengthwise along raw edge with Running Stitch, leaving open where marked.

16 Turn right side out. Stuff with polyester stuffing.

17 Turn one end of each sleeve in ½". Place hand in end of sleeve. Sew sleeve to hand with Running Stitch.

18 Sew sleeves to body with Ladder Stitch.

Sweater

19 Measure down 2" from top of sweater piece. Using fabric scissors, cut 1" slit on each side for armholes.

20 Pull sweater over body and push arms through armholes. Turn down top of sweater twice for collar and turn up bottom of sweater twice for ribbing.

Hat

21 Fold hat piece, with right sides together. Sew around raw edge with Gather Stitch. Pull gather to close. Knot to secure.

22 Turn right side out. Place hat on head and turn bottom edge up, forming brim.

Hands

12 Turn hands with right sides together. Sew around curved edge with Running Stitch, leaving open where marked.

13 Turn right side out. Stuff with polyester stuffing.

Kelsey

(Pictured at left on page 71.)
Materials & Tools on page 13
Blush
Satin ribbon: ⅛"-wide (30")
Socks: 1 pair, girl's size 6-9, anklet with ruffled
   edge and bows, white, for body, headband,
   pants, and tutu
Yarn: skein, for hair

Instructions

1 Begin by reading General Instructions on pages 5–13. Stitches and special techniques used are explained in this section.

2 Organize all materials and tools needed for project. Using fabric maker, mark cutting lines onto socks as shown in Diagrams A–B.

3 Using fabric scissors, cut out marked pieces from socks. Head and body are one piece.

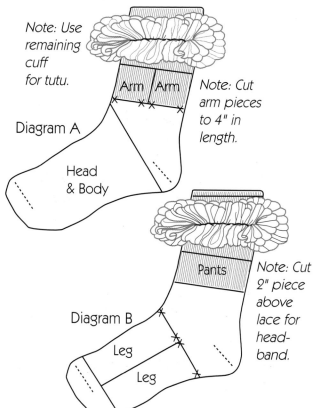

Note: Use remaining cuff for tutu.

Diagram A

Arm Arm

Note: Cut arm pieces to 4" in length.

Head & Body

Diagram B

Pants

Note: Cut 2" piece above lace for headband.

Leg

Leg

Head & Body

4 Sew around bottom of head with Gather Stitch.

5 Stuff toe firmly for head with polyester stuffing.

6 Pull gather to close. Knot to secure.

7 Sew over running stitch with Gather Stitch.

8 Stuff body piece firmly with polyester stuffing.

9 Sew across opening with Running Stitch.

10 Embroider eyes and mouth.

Arms

11 Fold each arm piece lengthwise, with right sides together. Sew lengthwise along raw edge with Running Stitch, leaving open where marked.

12 Sew across one end of each arm with Running Stitch, curving slightly to shape a rounded hand. Using fabric scissors, cut away excess sock.

13 Turn right side out. Stuff with polyester stuffing.

14 Sew arm to each side of body with Running Stitch.

Legs

15 Fold each leg piece lengthwise, with right sides together. Sew lengthwise along raw edge with Running Stitch, leaving open where marked.

16 Sew across one end of each leg with Running Stitch, curving slightly to shape a rounded foot.

17 Turn right side out. Stuff with polyester stuffing.

18 Sew leg ends closed. Sew legs to body with Ladder Stitch.

Pants

19 Fold pants piece, with right sides together. Sew pants, up 2" from end of leg, two stitches across to form crotch, and down other side with Running Stitch, as shown in Diagram C, leaving open where marked. Using fabric scissors, cut between seams.

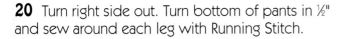

Diagram C

20 Turn right side out. Turn bottom of pants in ½" and sew around each leg with Running Stitch.

21 Place pants on body. Turn top of pants in ½" and sew to body with Running Stitch.

Tutu

22 Place tutu piece on body with ruffled edge facing down.

23 Turn top of piece in ½" and sew around waist with Ladder Stitch.

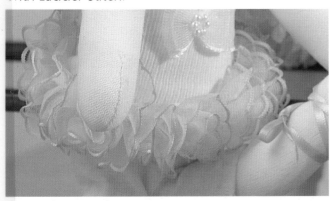

Headband

24 Turn outer edges of headband in ½" and place on head.

25 Sew headband to head with Running Stitch.

Hair

26 Using craft scissors, cut 5" x 6" piece from cardboard.

27 Wrap yarn around 5" width side of cardboard 16 times. Stick a threaded needle through middle of all strands and slide off, at the top of cardboard. Pull thread tight and sew to head (next to headband). Repeat, until hair is around entire headband.

28 Fill head with four additional bundles in middle of head. Trim ends to shape hair evenly. Leave hair loose.

Finish

29 Place ruffle around neck. Tack ends to back of neck.

30 Using fabric scissors, cut 15" of ribbon. Wrap ribbon around foot, crossing in front, back around ankle crossing in front. Knot. Tack in place to secure. Using remaining ribbon, repeat on other foot.

31 Using small paintbrush, brush blush lightly onto cheeks.

Tiny Dancer

(Pictured at right on page 71.)
Materials & Tools on page 13
Blush
Satin ribbon: ⅛"-wide (30")
Socks: 1 pair, toddler's size med, anklet with ruffled edge and bows, white, for body, headband, pants, and tutu
Yarn skein: for hair

Instructions
Assemble Tiny Dancer according to Kelsey's instructions and the additional instructions below.

Ponytail

1 Gather hair snug with ribbon for a ponytail. Tie into a bow.

Santa ♥

Materials & Tools on page 13

Blush

Felt: black (scrap)

Socks: 1 pair, crew, black, for belt, boots, and
mittens; 1 sock, crew, cream, for head; 1 pair,
crew, red, for body and hat; 1 pair, crew, terry,
white, for beard

Instructions

1 Begin by reading General Instructions on pages
5–13. Stitches and special techniques used are
explained in the General Instructions.

2 Organize all materials and tools needed for
project. Using fabric marker, mark cutting lines
onto socks as show in Diagrams A-G.

3 Using fabric scissors, cut out marked pieces
from socks.

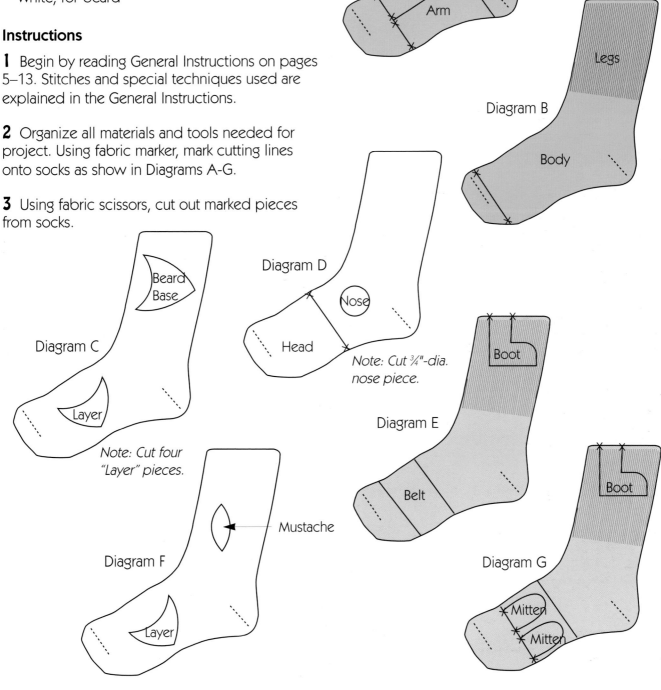

Diagram A — Hat, Arm, Arm

Diagram B — Legs, Body

Diagram C — Beard Base, Layer
Note: Cut four "Layer" pieces.

Diagram D — Nose, Head
Note: Cut ¾"-dia. nose piece.

Diagram E — Boot, Belt

Diagram F — Mustache, Layer

Diagram G — Boot, Mitten, Mitten

75

Head

4 Stuff head piece firmly with polyester stuffing. Head should be 3" in diameter.

5 Sew around opening with Gather Stitch. Pull gather to close. Knot to secure. Sculpt eye area of face.

6 Using fabric scissors, cut two ovals from black felt. Sew eyes to face.

Nose

7 Sew around edge of ¾"-dia. nose piece with Gather Stitch. Pull gather to close. Knot to secure. Repeat if nose needs to be smaller.

8 Sew nose to face with Ladder Stitch.

Body & Legs

9 Turn body piece wrong side out. Fold with heel seam facing up. Using straight pins, pin cuff to prevent sliding.

10 Sew up from edge ¼" right of center of cuff to end of cuff, four stitches across to form crotch, and back down to edge with Running Stitch as shown in Diagram H, leaving open where marked. Cut between leg seams.

Diagram H

11 Turn right side out and sew across bottom of legs with Running Stitch.

12 Legs are slender. Stuff bottom portion of each leg piece up 5" with polyester stuffing.

13 Sew across bend of each leg with Running Stitch, forming knees. Stuff each leg to top with polyester stuffing. Sew across top of legs with Running Stitch, forming joints between legs and body.

14 Stuff body piece firmly with polyester stuffing.

15 Sew around opening with Gather Stitch. Pull gather to close. Knot to secure.

16 Sew head to body with Ladder Stitch.

Arms & Mittens

17 Fold each arm piece lengthwise, with right sides together. Sew lengthwise along raw edge with Running Stitch, leaving open where marked.

18 Turn right side out. Stuff with polyester stuffing, leaving 1" on shoulder end unstuffed.

19 Turn mitten pieces, with right sides together. Sew along curved edges with Running Stitch, leaving open where marked.

20 Turn right side out. Stuff with polyester stuffing.

21 Sew openings closed with Running Stitch.

22 Turn end of each arm in ¼" and place mittens inside end of arms. Sew mittens to arms with Gather Stitch. Pull gather slightly. Knot to secure.

23 Sew arms to body with Ladder Stitch. They will be floppy.

Boots

24 Turn boot pieces, with right sides together. Sew along raw edges with Running Stitch, leaving open where marked.

25 Turn right side out. Stuff with polyester stuffing.

26 Turn top of each boot down ½", forming cuff. Place leg in boot. Sew to bottom of legs with Running Stitch.

Belt

27 Fold outer edges of belt to center. Place belt around belly. Sew belt to body with Running Stitch.

Beard & Mustache

28 Pull along bottom edge of beard base, stretching terry loops while sewing with Running Stitch.

29 Sew each layer, with looped side up. Sew top edge of Layer #1 over bottom edge of beard base with Running Stitch as shown in Diagram I.

30 Sew top edge of Layer #2 ¾" above stitching on Layer #1 with Running Stitch.

31 Sew top edge of Layer #3 ¾" above stitching on Layer #2 with Running Stitch. Repeat for Layer #4.

32 Sew beard to face with Running Stitch, curving around face.

33 Gather mustache in center and tack, with looped side up. Sew to face with center underneath nose.

Hat

34 Sew around tip of hat piece 1" from raw edge with Gather Stitch. Gather slightly. Knot to secure.

35 Tack end of hat to hat cuff. Sew hat to head with Running Stitch.

Finish

36 Using small paintbrush, brush blush lightly onto cheeks, mouth, and top of nose.

Witch

(Photo on page 78.)

Materials & Tools on page 13

Blush

Socks: 2 pairs, crew, black, for cape, hat, and shoes; 1 sock, crew, cream or green, for face, nose, and hands; 1 sock, crew, multicolor, for legs; 1 pair, crew, purple design, for body and sleeves

Instructions

1 Begin by reading General Instructions on pages 5–13. Stitches and special techniques used are explained in General Instructions.

2 Organize all materials and tools needed for project. Using fabric marker, mark cutting lines onto socks as shown in Diagrams A–H on pages 77 and 79.

Continued on page 79

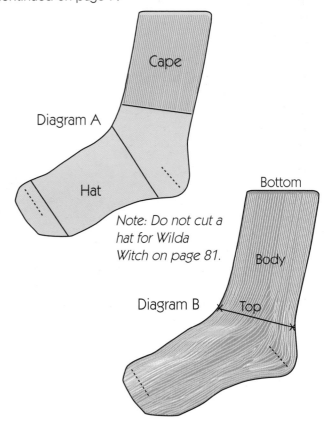

Diagram I

Beard

Layer #1

Diagram A

Cape

Hat

Note: Do not cut a hat for Wilda Witch on page 81.

Diagram B

Bottom

Body

Top

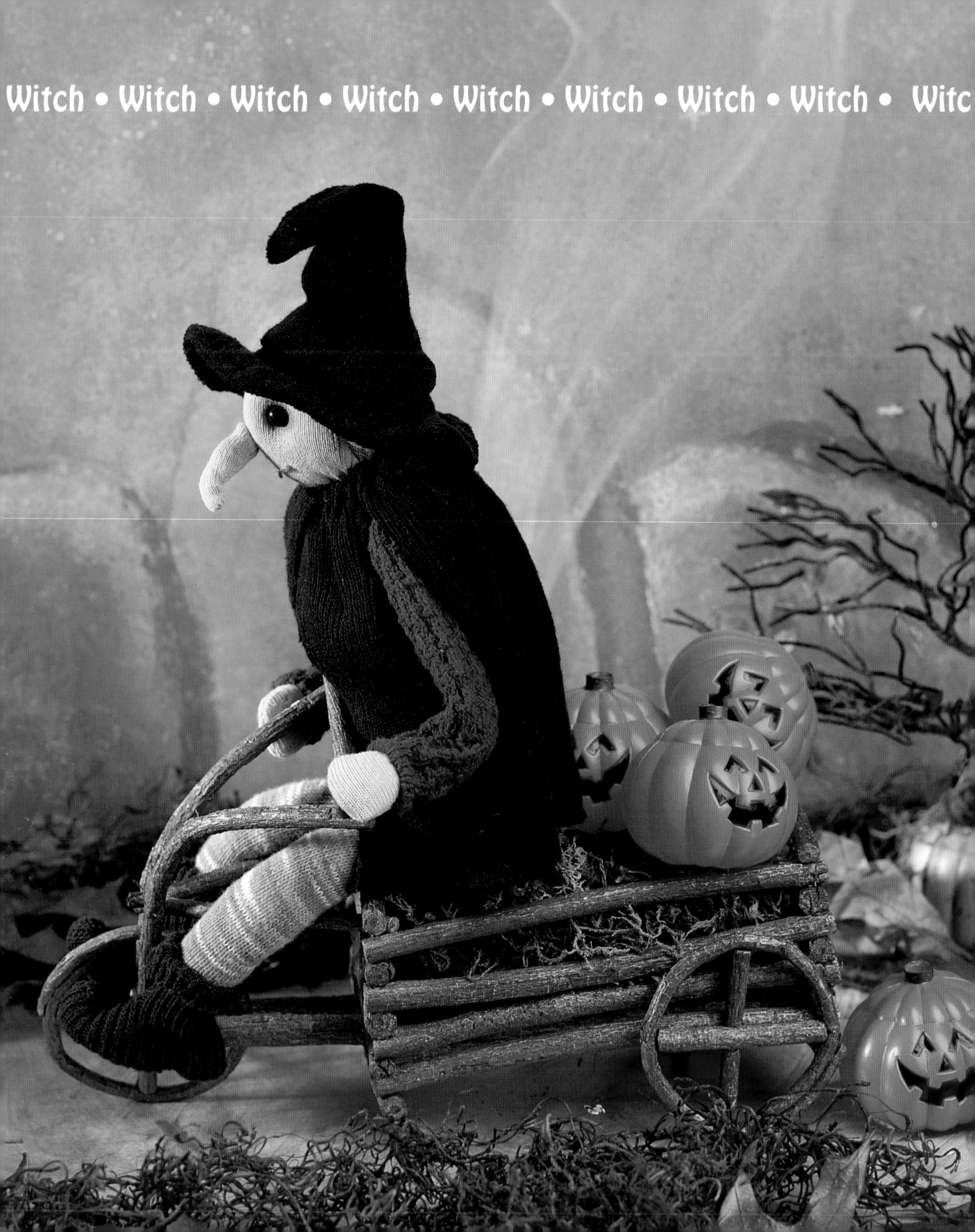

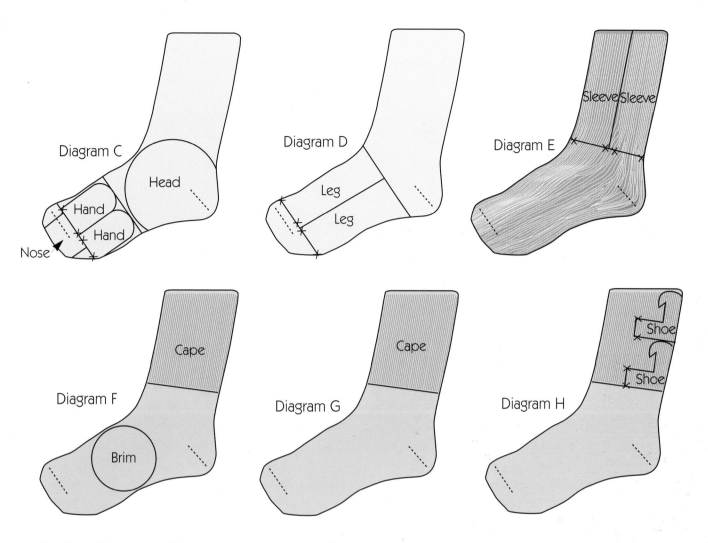

Diagram C — Head, Hand, Hand, Nose

Diagram D — Leg, Leg

Diagram E — Sleeve Sleeve

Diagram F — Cape, Brim

Diagram G — Cape

Diagram H — Shoe, Shoe

Continued from page 77.

3 Using fabric scissors, cut out marked pieces from socks.

Head & Face

4 Sew around opening of head piece with Gather Stitch. Pull slightly to gather.

5 Stuff head piece firmly with polyester stuffing.

6 Fold nose piece in half lengthwise, with right sides together. Sew nose with Running Stitch, as shown in Diagram I, leaving open where marked.
Using fabric scissors, cut away excess sock.

Diagram I

7 Turn right side out. Stuff lightly with polyester stuffing.

8 Turn open edge in and sew to face with Ladder Stitch. Make certain seam is down.

9 Sew along seam with three small Gather Stitches. Pull gather slightly to shape crooked nose. Knot to secure.

10 Sculpt eye area of face. Attach safety eyes to sculpted area. Embroider mouth onto face.

11 Pull gathers to close. Knot to secure.

Body

12 Sew around opening with Gather Stitch. Pull gather to close. Knot to secure.

13 Stuff body piece firmly with polyester stuffing.

14 Sew head to gathered end of body with Ladder Stitch.

Legs

15 Fold each leg piece lengthwise, with right sides together. Sew along lengthwise raw edge with Running Stitch, leaving open where marked.

16 Turn right side out. Stuff with polyester stuffing.

17 Sew across open end of legs with Running Stitch.

18 Place legs into bottom of body and sew across bottom of body with Running Stitch, securing legs to body.

Hands

19 Place hand pieces, with right sides together. Sew along curved edges with Running Stitch, leaving open where marked.

20 Turn right side out. Stuff with polyester stuffing.

21 Sew across open end of hands with Running Stitch.

Sleeves

22 Fold each sleeve piece lengthwise, with right sides together. Sew lengthwise along raw edge with Running Stitch, leaving open where marked.

23 Turn right side out. Turn one end of each sleeve in ¼" and place a hand in end of each sleeve. Sew hand to sleeve with Running Stitch.

24 Stuff with polyester stuffing.

25 Turn open end of each sleeve in ½". Sew to body with Ladder Stitch.

Cape

26 Fold cape pieces lengthwise, with right sides together. Sew lengthwise along raw edges of two pieces with Running Stitch, adjoining the three cape pieces, as shown in Diagram J.

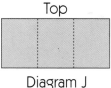

Top

Diagram J

27 Sew along top of cape with Gather Stitch.

28 Wrap gathered edge of cape around neck. Pull snugly to gather. Knot to secure. Using fabric marker, mark arm placement on cape. Using fabric scissors, cut two 2" slits, 1" from top edge. Pull arms through slits.

Shoes

29 Place shoe pieces, with right sides together. Sew along raw edges with Running Stitch, leaving open where marked.

30 Turn right side out. Stuff with polyester stuffing.

31 Place legs in shoes. Turn top of shoes down ½" and sew shoes to legs with Running Stitch.

32 Sew Loop Stitch in bottom of each shoe to define heel. Pull tight. Knot to secure.

Continued on page 82.

Continued from page 80.
Hat

33 Fold hat piece in half, with right sides together. Sew diagonally along length with Running Stitch, as shown in Diagram K, leaving open where marked. Using fabric scissors, cut away excess sock.

Diagram K

34 Turn right side out.

35 Place brim pieces, with right sides together. Sew around raw edges with Running Stitch. Using fabric scissors, cut 3" circle from center of brim.

36 Turn right side out.

37 Place open end of hat over 3" center in brim with right sides together. Sew hat to brim with Running Stitch. Sew ¼" in around edge of brim with Running Stitch.

38 Place hat on head. Sew hat to head with Running Stitch.

Wilda Witch

(Photo on page 81.)
Materials & Tools on page 13
Buttons: heart, small (4); round, small (8)
Hat: abaca, black
Heart charm
Mushroom bird: small
Plastic spider: small
Ribbon: mesh, 2"-wide (12"); satin, ½"-wide (12")
Socks: 2 pairs, crew, black, for cape and boots;
   1 sock, crew, cream, for face, nose, and hands;
   1 sock, crew, multicolor, for legs; 1 pair, crew,
   rose, for body and sleeves
Wire: 19-gauge, gold
Wire glasses
Wool: gray

Instructions

Assemble Wilda Witch according to Witch's instructions (except hat from Diagram A) and additional instructions below.

Hair & Hat

1 Arrange wool as desired on witch's head. Adhere wool to head with craft glue.

2 Adhere satin ribbon to hat with craft glue, creating hat band.

3 Adhere hat to head with craft glue.

4 Twist a piece of gold wire. Twist one end of twisted wire to tip of hat to secure. Twist heart charm to end.

Collar & Boots

5 Adhere mesh ribbon around neck for collar with craft glue.

6 Sew heart buttons down left front side of cape.

7 Adhere four round buttons to each boot with craft glue. See photo on page 81 for placement. Place buttons ½" apart.

8 Using wire cutters, cut four 1" pieces of wire. Adhere wires horizontally between buttons with craft glue.

9 Adhere spider to collar.

10 Adhere bird onto toe of boot.

Note: Wilda Witch has been surrounded by witchly items, such as a broom, a black cat, a toad, and lots of spiders for a more elaborate setting.

Snowman

(Photo on page 83.)

Materials & Tools on page 13

Blush

Cardboard: medium-weight

Felt: black (scrap)

Socks: 1 pair, child's size 6, white, for body and head; 1 sock, baby booty, white with striped cuff, for hat; 1 sock, crew, lt. blue, for scarf

Instructions

1 Begin by reading General Instructions on pages 5–13. Stitches and special techniques used are explained in the General Instructions.

2 Organize all materials and tools needed for project. Using fabric marker, mark cutting lines onto socks as shown in Diagrams A–C.

3 Using fabric scissors, cut out marked pieces from socks.

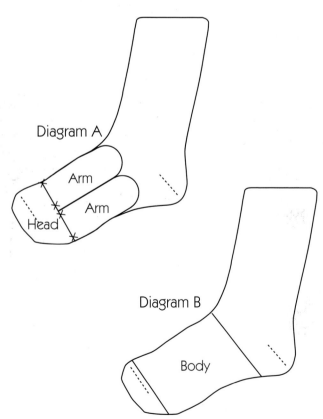

Diagram A

Arm

Arm

Head

Diagram B

Body

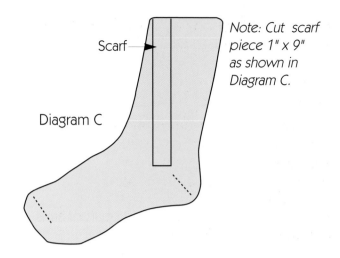

Scarf

Diagram C

Note: Cut scarf piece 1" x 9" as shown in Diagram C.

Head

4 Stuff head piece in desired shape with polyester stuffing. Head should be smaller than top of body.

5 Sew around opening with Gather Stitch. Pull gather to close.

6 Embroider eyes with French Knots. Embroider mouth.

Body

7 Sew around one end of body piece with Gather Stitch. Pull gather to close. Knot to secure.

8 Using craft scissors, cut 2" circle from medium weight cardboard. Place cardboard circle inside body and push down to gathered bottom.

9 Stuff ¾ of body firmly with polyester stuffing.

10 Sew around body up 2" from bottom with Gather Stitch. Pull to gather, forming a waist. Knot to secure.

11 Stuff remaining body firmly with polyester stuffing.

12 Sew around opening with Gather Stitch. Pull gather to close. Knot to secure.

13 Sew head to body with Ladder Stitch. Sew around again with Ladder Stitch.

Arms

14 Fold each arm piece lengthwise, with right sides together. Sew lengthwise along raw edge and across curved end of each arm with Running Stitch, leaving open where marked.

15 Turn right side out. Stuff lower part of arms with polyester stuffing.

16 Turn unstuffed arm ends in ¼" and sew to body with Ladder Stitch. Bend arms and tack to front of body.

Finish

17 Using fabric scissors, cut three small felt circles. Sew felt circles down middle for buttons.

18 Using small paintbrush, brush blush lightly onto cheeks.

19 Tie scarf around neck.

20 Place open end of baby bootie on top of head. Turn cuff up. Sew bootie to head with Running Stitch.

Mr. Shivers

(Photo on page 86.)
Materials & Tools on page 13
Acrylic paint: brown, gold, orange
Blush
Cardboard: medium-weight
Carpet tacks: black (2)
Dowel: ⅛"
Jingle bell: 10 mm, gold
Pencil sharpener
Socks: 1 sock, crew, lt. green, for tree; 1 pair, crew, dk. green, for hat and tree; 1 sock, crew, red, for scarf; 1 pair, men's, crew, white, terry, for body
Wire: 19-gauge, black, gold
Wood star: 1"

Instructions

Assemble Mr. Shivers according to Snowman's instructions (except Diagram C) and the additional instructions listed below. Refer to Diagram A–C for scarf, hat, and tree. *Note: Turn men's white terry crew socks, so looped side becomes right side.*

1 Using fabric marker, mark cutting lines onto socks as shown in Diagrams A-B.

2 Using fabric scissors, cut out marked pieces from socks.

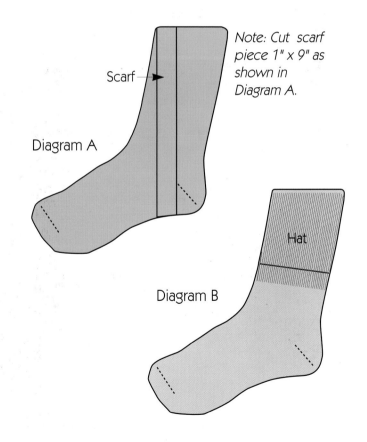

Scarf →

Note: Cut scarf piece 1" x 9" as shown in Diagram A.

Diagram A

Hat

Diagram B

Continued on page 87.

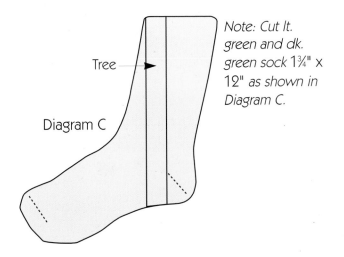

Tree →

Diagram C

Note: Cut lt. green and dk. green sock 1¾" x 12" as shown in Diagram C.

Continued from page 85.

Tree

3 Using wire cutters, cut 6½" piece from dowel. Using small paintbrush, paint dowel with brown acrylic paint.

4 Fold tree strip in half lengthwise with right sides together. Cut slits along lengthwise raw edges of each strip to within ¼" of fold as shown in Diagram E.

Diagram E

5 Cover 3½" on one end of painted dowel with craft glue. Hold strips together and twist around glued end of dowel, beginning in middle and ending at top to form tree.

6 Adhere a jingle bell to top of tree with craft glue. Apply glue to tree trunk and push through bend of arm, holding in place while glue dries.

Hat

7 Place hat piece on snowman's head. Turn cuff up and sew hat to head with Running Stitch.

8 Paint wood star with gold acrylic paint. Let dry.

9 Using wire cutters, cut 6" piece from gold wire and twist around top of hat, 1" from end.

10 Using needle nose pliers, curl wire into small loops. Wrap end of wire around star and twist end to secure.

Finish

11 Dip pointed ends of carpet tacks in glue and push into face for eyes.

12 Using pencil sharpener, sharpen end of dowel, measure 1" length, and cut other end. Paint with orange acrylic paint. Let dry.

13 Dip cut end of painted dowel in glue and push into face for nose.

14 Using wire cutters, cut 2" piece of black wire.

15 Using needle nose pliers, shape wire into mouth. Bend ends of mouth. Dip ends in craft glue and push into face.

16 Using wire cutters, cut three 2" pieces of black wire.

17 Using needle nose pliers, shape spiral discs. Bend outside end of each spiral. Dip each end in glue and push into center of body for button.

18 Tie scarf around neck.

19 Using small paintbrush, brush blush lightly onto cheeks.

Note: Mr. Shivers has been placed in front of a wooden picket fence that is surrounded by fabric trees, a clothes line with winter mittens, and a bundle of snowballs for a more elaborate setting.

Cat ♥

Materials & Tools on page 13

Fabric: 1"-wide (16")
Socks: 1 pair, crew, pink, for body

Instructions

1 Begin by reading General Instructions on pages 5–13. Stitches and special techniques used are explained in the General Instructions.

2 Organize all materials and tools needed for project. Using fabric marker, mark cutting lines onto socks as shown in Diagrams A-B.

3 Using fabric scissors, cut out marked pieces from socks.

Head

4 Sew around opening of head piece with Gather Stitch. Pull slightly to gather, leaving unsecured.

88

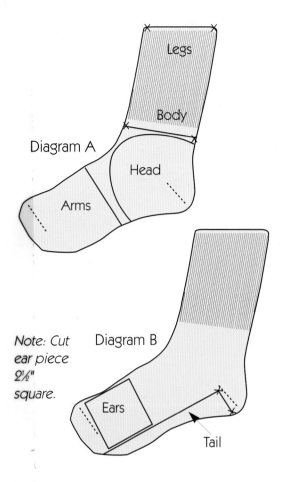

Diagram A

Legs

Body

Head

Arms

Note: Cut ear piece 2½" square.

Diagram B

Ears

Tail

5 Stuff head firmly with polyester stuffing. (Heel is face.)

6 Sculpt eye area of face. Attach safety eyes to sculpted area.

7 Sculpt nose between eyes. Attach safety nose to sculpted area.

8 Pull gather to close. Knot to secure.

Ears

9 Fold each ear piece in half diagonally, with right sides together, forming a triangle. Sew one raw edge with Running Stitch.

10 Turn right side out. Sew across openings with Ladder Stitch. Sew over Ladder Stitch with Gather Stitch. Pull slightly to gather. Knot to secure.

11 Sew gathered side of ears to head with Ladder Stitch.

Body & Legs

12 Fold body and legs piece, with right sides together. Sew top of cuff closed with Running Stitch, creating bottom of leg.

13 Turn right side out. Stuff firmly with polyester stuffing.

14 Sew around opening with Gather Stitch. Pull gather to close. Knot to secure.

15 Sew from center of cuff up 2½" with Running Stitch, going through both layers. Pull thread tight to define legs.

16 Sew bottom of each leg with a tight Loop Stitch to form a toe. Repeat for five toes at end of each leg.

17 Sew head to body with Ladder Stitch.

Arms

18 Fold arm piece, with toe seam on top. Cut as shown in Diagram C, creating two pieces.

Diagram C

19 Fold arm pieces lengthwise, with right sides together. Sew lengthwise along raw edges with Running Stitch, leaving open where marked in Diagram C.

20 Turn right side out. Stuff with polyester stuffing.

21 Sew toe seam end with Loop Stitch, forming fingers. Repeat for five fingers at end of each arm.

22 Sew arms to body with Ladder Stitch. Toe seam on fingers should be facing down.

Tail

23 Fold tail piece lengthwise, with right sides together. Sew lengthwise along raw edge with Running Stitch, leaving open where marked. Taper end of tail toward toe seam.

24 Turn right side out. Stuff with polyester stuffing.

25 Sew tail to back of body above leg seam with Ladder Stitch.

Finish

26 Using small paintbrush, brush blush lightly onto cheeks and inside of ears.

27 Wrap fabric strip around neck. Tie into bow and tack bow to secure.

Doll with Bonnet

(Pictured in center on page 88.)
Materials & Tools on page 13
Blush
Socks: 1 pair, crew, cream or white, for
    body; 2 pairs, crew, pink, for bonnet, dress,
    neck ruffle, panties, sleeves, and shoes

Instructions

1 Begin by reading General Instructions on pages 5–13. Stitches and special techniques used are explained in the General Instructions.

2 Organize all materials and tools needed for project. Using marking pen, mark cutting lines onto socks as shown in Diagrams A–F.

3 Using fabric scissors, cut out marked pieces from socks.

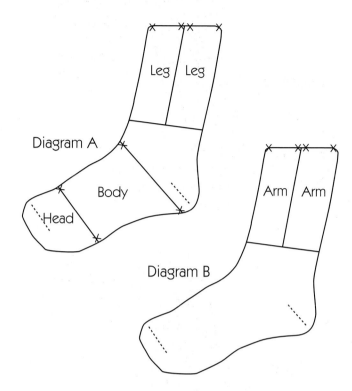

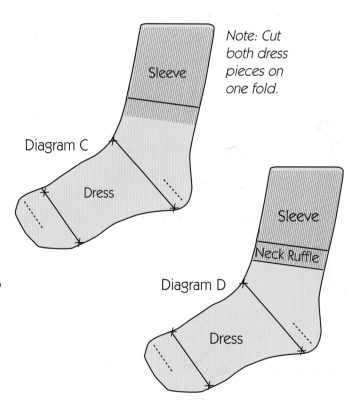

Note: Cut both dress pieces on one fold.

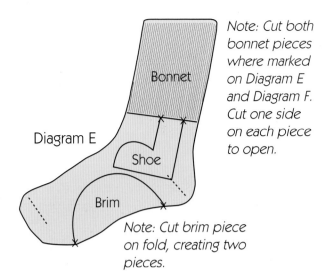

Diagram E

Bonnet

Shoe

Brim

Note: Cut both bonnet pieces where marked on Diagram E and Diagram F. Cut one side on each piece to open.

Note: Cut brim piece on fold, creating two pieces.

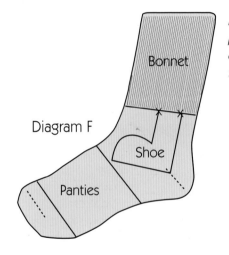

Diagram F

Bonnet

Shoe

Panties

Note: Cut panties piece on fold, creating two pieces.

Head

4 Stuff head piece firmly with polyester stuffing.

5 Embroider eyes onto face.

6 Sew around opening with Gather Stitch. Pull gather to close. Knot to secure.

Body

7 Sew around one open end with Gather Stitch. Pull gather to close. Knot to secure.

8 Stuff body firmly with polyester stuffing.

9 Sew head to gathered end of body with Ladder Stitch.

Legs

10 Fold each leg piece lengthwise, with right sides together. Sew lengthwise along raw edges and across one end with Running Stitch, leaving open where marked.

11 Turn right side out. Stuff with polyester stuffing.

12 Sew across open ends with Running Stitch.

13 Place legs in bottom opening of body. Sew across opening with Running Stitch to secure legs to body.

Shoes

14 Place shoe pieces, with right sides together. Sew along edges with Running Stitch, leaving open where marked.

15 Turn right side out. Stuff bottom of shoes with polyester stuffing.

16 Place leg into each shoe. Sew shoe to each leg, down ½" from top, with Running Stitch. Turn down top of each shoe.

Panties

17 Place panties pieces, with right sides together. Using fabric scissors, cut as shown in Diagram F. Sew panties together along curved edge with Running Stitch.

Diagram F

18 Keeping right sides together. Match seams and sew inside leg seam from bottom end of one leg to other leg with Running Stitch, forming legs of panties.

19 Turn right side out. Place on doll. Turn bottom on panties up ¼" and sew around edges with Running Stitch.

20 Turn top of panties down ¼". Secure to body with Running Stitch.

Arms

21 Place arm pieces with right sides together. Sew lengthwise along raw edges, rounding end to form hand-shape, leaving open where marked.

22 Using fabric scissors, cut away excess sock from seam.

23 Turn right side out. Stuff with polyester stuffing.

24 Sew across open ends with Running Stitch.

Sleeves

25 Slip sleeve piece onto each arm. Sew bottom of sleeve ½" up from sleeve cuff end with Gather Stitch. Pull hand out 1½". Pull gather snugly around arm. Knot to secure.

26 Sew arm to sleeve with Running Stitch.

27 Sew arm only down ½" on each side of body, with Ladder Stitch.

28 Sew around top edge of sleeve with Gather Stitch. Pull slightly to gather. Knot to secure.

29 Sew sleeve to body, with Ladder Stitch.

Dress

30 Place dress pieces, with right sides together. Sew lengthwise along raw edges with Running Stitch, leaving open where marked.

31 Turn right side out. Sew top of dress with

Gather Stitch. Place dress on body, with seams on sides. Pull thread to gather snugly around neck. Knot to secure.

32 Measure down ½" from top of both seams and cut 2" slit next to each seam for armholes. Pull arms through dress.

33 Take 1" at bottom edge of dress and pull tightly to stretch. Repeat around entire bottom edge for ruffles. Sew along bottom edge with Running Stitch, to keep edges from fraying.

Neck Ruffle

34 Take 1" at bottom edge of neck piece and pull tightly to stretch. Repeat around entire bottom edge for ruffles.

35 Sew top edge with Gather Stitch, leaving unsecured. Place around neck and pull thread snugly to gather. Knot to secure.

Bonnet

36 Place brim pieces, with right sides together. Sew along curved edge with Running Stitch, leaving open where marked.

37 Turn right side out. Sew in ¼" along curved edge with Running Stitch.

38 Place bonnet pieces, with right sides together. Sew together along one edge with Running Stitch.

39 Using fabric marker, draw shape as shown in Diagram G.

40 Using fabric scissors, cut out shape. Do not cut on fold.

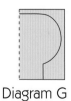

Diagram G

41 Open bonnet and sew along curved edge with Gather Stitch. Pull gather to fit brim.

42 Sew gathered edge of bonnet to brim, with right sides together, with Running Stitch.

43 Stuff bonnet lightly with polyester stuffing.

44 Place bonnet on head. Sew back edge of bonnet to head. Sew bonnet to head along gather.

Finish

45 Using fabric scissors, cut 1" x 3" piece of cardboard. Wrap embroidery floss around 1" side of cardboard 18 times. Tie thread around floss. Knot to secure. Repeat for five bundles.

46 Sew bundles of floss to head under brim with Running Stitch.

Mattie

(Pictured at left on page 88.)
Materials & Tools on page 13
Blush
Socks: 1 pair, crew, cream or white, for body; 1 sock, crew, pink, for collar and pants; 1 sock, crew, lavender, for shirt, sleeves, and shoes; 1 sock, crew, yellow, for hair

Instructions

Assemble Mattie according to Doll's instructions and the additional instructions listed below. Follow Dress instructions on page 92 for shirt. Refer to Diagrams A–C below for marking and cutting, shirt, shoes, collar, and hair.

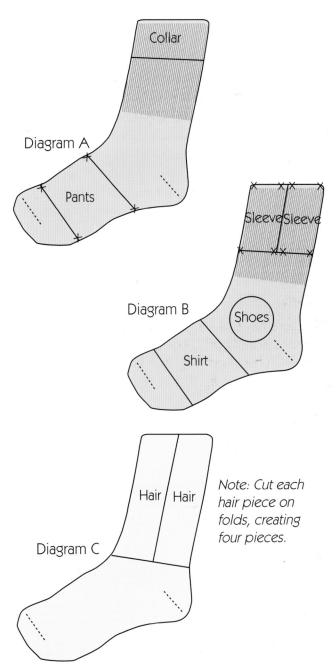

Note: Cut each hair piece on folds, creating four pieces.

Shoes

1 Turn raw edge of each circle in ¼". Sew around edge with Gather Stitch.

2 Place circle around each foot. Pull thread snugly to gather around bottom of foot, for shoe.

3 Sew shoes to feet with Running Stitch.

Sleeves

4 Fold each sleeve piece lengthwise, with wrong sides together. Sew lengthwise along raw edge of each sleeve with Running Stitch, leaving open where marked.

5 Turn wrong side out. Place an arm in each sleeve of dress. Place a sleeve and arm through each armhole.

6 Sew each arm and sleeve to body with Ladder Stitch.

7 Turn edge of each sleeve in ¼". Sew around with Running Stitch.

Collar

8 Fold outer edges to center for collar. Place collar around neck.

Hair

9 Fold hair pieces in half lengthwise. Using fabric scissors, cut ¼" slits along lengthwise raw edges of each piece to within ¼" of fold as shown in Diagram D.

Diagram D

10 Sew middle of one hair piece across top front of head, from side to side, with Running Stitch.

11 Sew the middle of one hair piece across bottom back of head, from side to side, with Running Stitch.

12 Sew middle of the two remaining hair pieces in between top and bottom pieces, from side to side, with Running Stitch.

Finish

13 Place finger at base of each strip and with other finger pull and stretch each strip carefuly.

Wings ♥

Wings are necessary for the Angels and Bees projects, but can be added to any project as desired.

Materials & Tools on page 13
Cardboard: lightweight
Quilt batting: thin
Socks: 1 pair, crew, color of choice, for wings

Instructions

1 Begin by reading General Instructions on pages 5–13. Stitches and special techniques used are explained in the General Instructions.

2 Enlarge Wings Pattern 140% at a copy center.

3 Organize all materials and tools needed for project. Trace pattern onto cardboard for template. Using craft scissors, cut out wings.

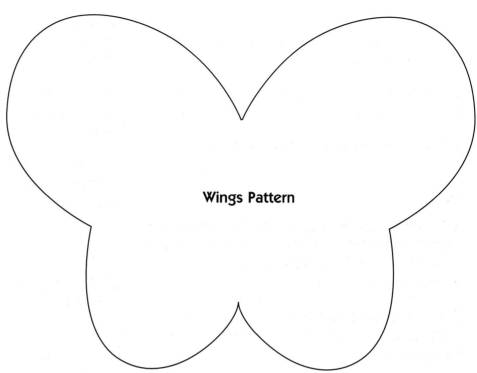

Wings Pattern

Diagram A

Wings

4 Using fabric marker, mark cutting lines onto socks as shown in Diagram A.

5 Using fabric scissors, cut out marked pieces from socks.

6 Cut one fold on each sock to open. Lay wing pieces flat, with right sides together.

7 Cut a piece of batting same size as sock pieces and lay under socks. Pin all three pieces together.

8 Lay wings template on top of socks. Using fabric marker, trace wings onto socks.

9 Sew batting and socks together, along traced pattern, with Running Stitch. Using fabric scissors, cut away excess sock to within ¼" of stitching.

10 Cut 1" slit in top sock only, leaving other sock and batting in tact. Turn wings right side out through slit.

11 Using stuffing tool, push all seams out to shape. Sew slit closed with Ladder Stitch.

12 Sew around wings ¼" from edge with Running Stitch.

13 Tack wings to body with slit against body.

Metric Conversion Chart

mm-millimetres cm-centimetres
inches to millimetres and centimetres

inches	mm	cm	inches	cm	inches	cm
⅛	3	0.3	9	22.9	30	76.2
¼	6	0.6	10	25.4	31	78.7
½	13	1.3	12	30.5	33	83.8
⅝	16	1.6	13	33.0	34	86.4
¾	19	1.9	14	35.6	35	88.9
⅞	22	2.2	15	38.1	36	91.4
1	25	2.5	16	40.6	37	94.0
1¼	32	3.2	17	43.2	38	96.5
1½	38	3.8	18	45.7	39	99.1
1¾	44	4.4	19	48.3	40	101.6
2	51	5.1	20	50.8	41	104.1
2½	64	6.4	21	53.3	42	106.7
3	76	7.6	22	55.9	43	109.2
3½	89	8.9	23	58.4	44	111.8
4	102	10.2	24	61.0	45	114.3
4½	114	11.4	25	63.5	46	116.8
5	127	12.7	26	66.0	47	119.4
6	152	15.2	27	68.6	48	121.9
7	178	17.8	28	71.1	49	124.5
8	203	20.3	29	73.7	50	127.0

Index